Kawaii
Resin & Clay Workshop

✳ Crafting Super-Cute Charms, Miniatures, Figures & More ✳

Alex Lee, **Creator of Polymomo Tea**

✳ I dedicate this book to my family and friends,
who always encouraged my hobby and passion for crafting.
Also, a big shout-out to all the crafters who helped the
PolymomoTea brand grow, which allowed me to publish this book. ✳

Inspiring | Educating | Creating | Entertaining

Brimming with creative inspiration, how-to projects, and useful information to enrich your everyday life, Quarto Knows is a favorite destination for those pursuing their interests and passions. Visit our site and dig deeper with our books into your area of interest: Quarto Creates, Quarto Cooks, Quarto Homes, Quarto Lives, Quarto Drives, Quarto Explores, Quarto Gifts, or Quarto Kids.

Design and presentation © 2020 Quarto Publishing Group USA Inc.
Text and projects © 2020 Alex Lee

First Published in 2020 by Quarry Books, an imprint of The Quarto Group,
100 Cummings Center, Suite 265-D, Beverly, MA 01915, USA.
T (978) 282-9590 F (978) 283-2742 QuartoKnows.com

Quarry Books titles are also available at discount for retail, wholesale, promotional, and bulk purchase. For details, contact the Special Sales Manager by email at specialsales@quarto.com or by mail at The Quarto Group,
Attn: Special Sales Manager, 100 Cummings Center, Suite 265-D, Beverly, MA 01915, USA.

10 9 8 7 6 5 4 3 2 1

ISBN: 978-1-63159-968-2

Digital edition published in 2020
eISBN: 978-1-63159-969-9

Library of Congress Cataloging-in-Publication Data is available.

Design: Rita Sowins / Sowins Design
Cover Image: Glenn Scott Photography
Page Layout: Rita Sowins / Sowins Design
Photography: Alex Lee and Glenn Scott Photography on pages 1, 3, 6, 26 (right), 30 (right), 33 (bottom), 34 (left),
45 (bottom right), 51 (bottom), 57 (bottom), 61 (bottom right), 65 (bottom), 69 (bottom), 72 (left), 76 (right), 80 (right), 83 (bottom), 84 (left), 88 (left), 105 (bottom), 113 (bottom), 121 (bottom), 122 (bottom), 130 (bottom), 135, 139 (bottom), 140, and 144

Printed in China

Contents

Introduction

Sculpting is a form of art that involves the creation of a three-dimensional piece. Some sculptors work with pottery, some work with stone, but I like to work with polymer clay and resin. Sometimes, working with one type of material restricts the details the piece can portray. For me, working with clay meant sacrificing translucence. I always liked the clear crispness of glasswork. I am no glass-blower, so I incorporated resin, which is much easier to handle than glass.

Crafting has always been a hobby for me. Inexpensive and engaging, it also relieved my stress. There's a kind of euphoria when you look at a finished product after hours of work—a sense of accomplishment. To be honest, I don't need a reason to craft. I just like working with my hands and letting my imagination come into the 3D world.

I didn't start with mixed media. My crafting journey started with making miniature sculptures and keychains out of polymer clay. A few years later, I experimented with making large pieces out of two-part resin, but making a finished piece took a long time: I had to place a base layer; wait until it was tacky; place in a sticker, which was the trend back in the day; then place glitter; wait a day for the first layer to cure; then pour a second layer of resin for the background. It was a two-day process. Then my friend introduced me to UV resin, my preferred resin. I started incorporating resin into my clay pieces, first using it as a glaze and then making my own silicone molds to create pieces with a translucent look, and I continued on from there.

One thing I would like to emphasize before we start is to not focus on trying to make your sculptures exactly like the photos you see in this book. Sculpting is a form of art and creation, and by sculpting in good earnest fun, you are already adding your own creative spin on it. The more it differs from my version, the more it will reflect your own art style. Also, if you don't like the way it looks, you can remake it. I have been sculpting for over a decade, and I often cringe when I look at my early work. But I also love seeing the progress from where I was then to where I am now. I sometimes think the rougher-looking, cringe-inducing pieces I made in the past show more artistic flare and creativity than those I make now.

People often ask about my sources of inspiration. I am inspired by everyday life. I use basic, everyday objects—animals and things I see in the environment—and think of a way to make them into cute little figures using clay and resin. My art style can be classified as "kawaii," which is the Japanese term for "cute." My interpretation of kawaii is an adorable caricature of an animal, object, or place. I always start with a resin or clay base and build up from there.

Before we get started, I'd like to thank everyone who took the time to pick up this book in a store or online. In these pages, there are twenty-five unique tutorials that I have created with my favorite mixture of crafting: resin, clay, and cuteness.

I promise you: If you like working with your hands, experimenting with your creativity, and combining different art mediums, this is the book and hobby for you.

1

Essential
Supplies &
Techniques

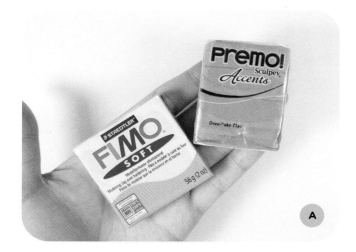

A

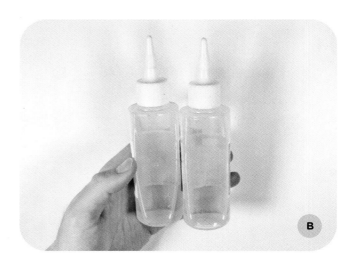

B

C

D

E

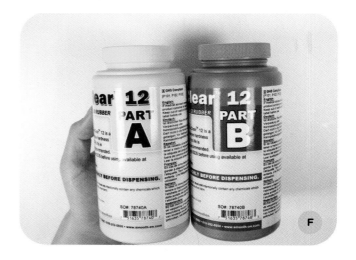

F

Basic Tools & Materials

This hobby requires an initial investment in supplies, but they can last for a long time. I'm still trying to use up the clay I bought years ago.

POLYMER CLAY (A) is an oven-bake clay, meaning that when it's baked according to the manufacturer's instructions it will cure and harden. Brands I particularly like to use are Sculpey, Sculpey Premo!, and Fimo.

As its name implies, **TWO-PART RESIN (B)** comes in two parts that you mix together, typically at a 1:1, 1:2, or 1:3 ratio. This is probably the most common type of resin.

Unlike UV resin, two-part resin cures over time—from six to forty-eight hours, depending on the brand. If this is the resin you choose, you can pour it, neglect it for a day, and continue to craft some more. Two-part resin is great for bigger projects, and it's less expensive per volume than UV resin.

UV RESIN (C) cures when it's exposed to UV light. Unlike two-part resin, UV resin doesn't have to be mixed. I use a UV nail lamp to cure my UV resin.

While working with or storing UV resin, keep it out of direct sunlight or strong lighting systems, which could cause it to harden or cure prematurely. UV resin can be used in several ways: to add details to a piece, to create a nice glossy layer of glaze, and even as a glue.

UV LAMP (D) choices vary from handheld to stationary. I use a 36-watt lamp, shown here, which is made for curing nail art. You need to cure UV resin layer by layer. Depending on thickness and amount of pigment, I cure each piece between one and two minutes, flip it, and cure it again.

PIGMENTS (E) are colored ink extracts that you mix into UV resin to provide color. There are many types of pigments that can be added: transparent, opaque, pearlescent, and glitter. I like to add in small amounts of pigment at a time, making sure I don't add too much, especially when using opaque pigments. The opacity added to the UV resin prevents light from traveling through the resin, so it won't cure. When curing opaque pigments, I make sure that I add thin layers and cure each layer separately, which will reduce the risk of resin not curing completely.

I use a **TWO-PART MOLD-MAKING PRODUCT (F)** to create custom molds for my projects. I like Sorta-Clear 12 because in twelve hours it cures completely to a semi-translucent finish that allows light to penetrate and cure the UV resin. The greater the mold maker's opacity, the less UV light can travel through it, reducing the likelihood that the resin will cure. If the mold maker you like is opaque, use two-part resin, which cures over time rather than with light.

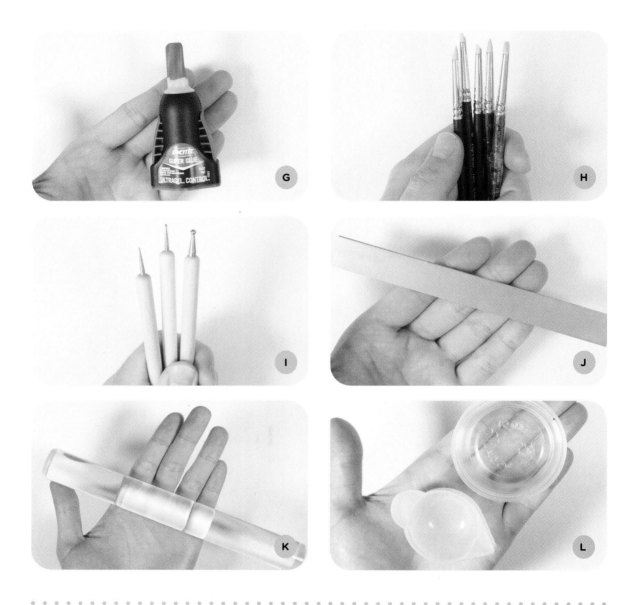

UV resin sticks to clay and can adhere resin pieces to each other, but I feel the gel type of **SUPER GLUE (G)** gives superior control and avoids slippage. Little dots of super glue gel dry within seconds without mess.

I have found silicone clay sculpture tools, dotting tools (usually used for nail art), a polymer clay blade, and a clay roller **(H-K)** to be useful tools. I also use **silicone cups, plastic containers (L),** popsicle sticks, glitter, tape, paintbrushes, toothpicks, and other supplies to complete my projects.

Techniques & Methods

There are endless ways to use polymer clay and resin, especially if you add other materials. In this section, I share the most basic techniques to get you started. Useful tutorials include making a silicone mold and working with UV resin. UV resin is a fairly new material in mainstream crafting; most people are familiar with two-part resin, which requires a curing time of up to twenty-four hours. Fortunately, UV resin has a wait time of only a few minutes, allowing us to finish our crafting projects more quickly.

Safety Tips & Tricks

Before you start working on any of the projects, I would like to remind you that **both UV and two-part resin are chemical compounds.** Be sure to exercise caution and care when working with these products.

In addition, **please refer to the manufacturer's descriptions, safety information, and instructions for all materials before using them.** I can share my tips and tricks, but your products and the companies that manufactured them will be able to give you information about the product, the chemicals, and safe usage.

When using any type of resin, wear gloves and long sleeves to protect your skin. Resin may cause irritation or even allergic reactions when it comes in contact with the skin.

Make sure that your crafting area is well-ventilated. Open a window and turn on a fan, preferably a ceiling fan to allow air to circulate and minimize any fumes from resin or polymer clay as they're curing.

When working with resin and mold-making products, **it's strongly recommended that you also wear safety goggles/glasses and a mask, ideally one with a respirator in it, to avoid inhaling any fumes.**

To protect your work surface and workspace, **cover all your surfaces before working with resin.** For example, a silicone mat offers good surface protection.

Working with Kids

For adults who would like to work on these projects with children: While it's fine for kids to mold and shape polymer clay, **adults should handle all the other processes and materials: oven-curing the polymer clay, making molds, and working with resin.** Polymer clay is safe for kids to handle, but resin crafting and moldmaking require care and attention, so they're best left to adults.

Making a Mold

Probably the most important part of my journey in combining resin and polymer clay art is being able to create my own silicone molds. Here are the steps I use to make them.

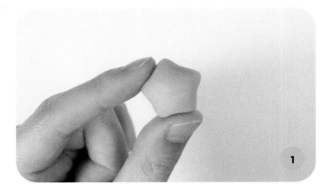

1. Make a template—a polymer clay sculpture or another piece that you've already cured in the oven and will use to make a mold. I usually use scrap pieces of clay for this. Once you've cured the clay template according to the manufacturer's instructions, let it cool completely before using it to make a mold.

2. Find a container large enough to surround the polymer clay template; it will also define the overall shape of the mold. I like to use a circular container, such as the small plastic one shown. (Note that I cut out the bottom because the silicone mold would have picked up the writing inscribed on the plastic. If your container doesn't have any patterns or lettering on it, you probably can get away with not cutting off the bottom.) Other good mold containers are paper cups, cookie cutters, and storage containers.

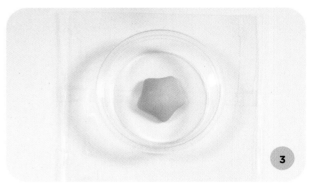

3. Place a piece of packing tape sticky side up on a flat work surface. Gently press the clay template onto the tape to keep any silicone from slipping under it. I also press the open container bottom onto the tape to seal it.

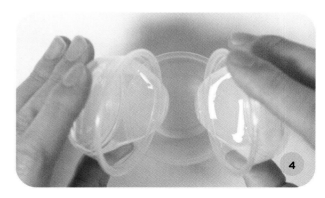

How Long Should I Mix?

I like to use streak marks as an indicator. When you first combine parts A and B, there are lines that show the two different materials together. I keep stirring until I don't see that distinction between the two parts. So basically, I mix until it's one giant gloop.

4. Sorta-Clear 12 is my silicone mold-making product of choice. Of course, you may use any brand you prefer, but I like that particular one because it cures very clear, permitting UV light to penetrate, thus allowing UV resin to cure. (If you use an opaque product, you can still follow this tutorial, but you'll need to use the finished mold with two-part resin, which cures over time rather than with UV light.) Sorta-Clear uses a 1:1 ratio of two parts, A and B. Measure out an equal amount of each and pour both into a larger bowl.

5. Stir the mixture slowly to prevent too many bubbles from forming. Stirring too vigorously introduces air into the mixture, trapping it beneath the silicone.

6. Pour the fully combined mixture onto the clay template. I try to make enough mixture to submerge the clay template at least 5 mm from the surface and 1 cm on the sides. If the mold is too thin, the weight of the resin can deform the mold.

7. Wait for the mold to cure completely, which may take six to twenty-four hours, depending on the product. If you're uncertain of the timing, wait a day. Once the material sets, remove the container and tape from the mold. Carefully remove the clay template. The completed mold is now ready to fill with resin.

Adding Pigments to Resin

When coloring UV resin, I like to use translucent pigment, which cures better than opaque pigment. If I plan to use opaque pigment, I add only a very small amount to the UV resin. Then I cure in multiple thin layers, because UV light can't penetrate through opaque pigmentation; it will only cure the surface. Two-part resin doesn't depend on light to cure, so I can freely add more opaque pigment to it.

1. Pour some UV resin into a silicone cup. Because resin doesn't permanently stick to them once cured, silicone cups, such as cupcake liners, are perfect because they're reusable and easy to clean.

2. Add a small dot of liquid coloring pigment to your resin. Adding too much pigment will interfere with the properties of resin, especially UV resin, preventing it from properly curing. If, after curing under the UV lamp for a long time, the resin still has a sticky residue, you may have added too much liquid pigment. While you should take similar care with two-part resin, it can handle more pigment than UV resin.

3. Slowly stir the mixture with a toothpick to prevent air bubbles from getting trapped in the resin.

4. Continue to mix until you see a homogenous-colored resin. If using two-part resin, feel free to liberally add glitters and other pieces into the resin mixture; add these embellishments in moderation if using UV resin to again ensure the UV light can penetrate.

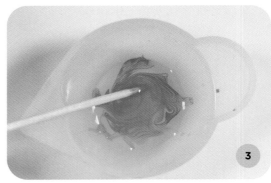

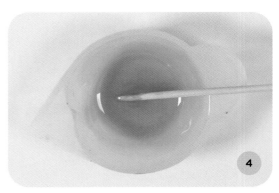

Curing UV Resin

Curing the UV resin is the most satisfying for me. I personally don't like to wait twenty-four hours for my resin to cure, so a few minutes under UV light is perfect for an impatient guy like me!

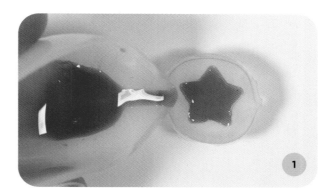

1. Pour your UV resin mixture into a silicone mold.

2. Place it under the UV lamp for two to three minutes. Some instructions say thirty seconds is enough, but I recommend a longer time: There's no such thing as over-curing, but under-curing will leave a sticky, slimy residue on the piece. After the resin has finished curing, flip over the piece and cure it under the UV lamp for another two to three minutes. Because there's always the chance the UV light didn't penetrate the piece, it doesn't hurt to add an extra cure. My general rule is: The more sides a piece has, the more cures I do, especially with dark-colored pigments. Also, it's helpful to do an extra cure after taking the piece out of the mold.

3. Upon finishing the series of extra cures, carefully take the piece out of the mold.

Glazing with UV Resin

Glazing adds a shiny finish to the piece. Personally, I prefer this to a matte texture. The gloss-finish products I once used took a long time to dry and required multiple layers to achieve the finish I was after. Now I rely on UV resin because it usually requires only one layer of glaze and cures within a few minutes under a UV lamp.

1. Place your resin piece on a silicone mat or the underside of a mold to protect your work surface. Dip a paintbrush into the UV resin. I like to use the cheapest paintbrush I have because, even with careful cleaning, the resin ruins the bristles after a few uses.

2. Paint a thin layer of UV resin onto the piece. For a simple piece, such as this star, I like to brush on my resin in one layer. On a more intricate piece, I brush on the resin one component at a time and lightly cure between each component. This more controlled method prevents excess resin from dripping on the sides.

3. Cure the piece under a UV lamp for a few minutes to complete the glaze. The star on the left is unglazed and the star on the right is glazed. I like the shinier star much better. UV resin is perfect for giving a glassy look to resin pieces and adding an extra shine to polymer clay pieces.

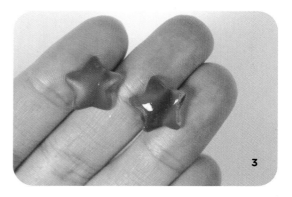

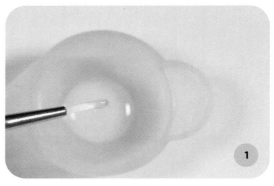

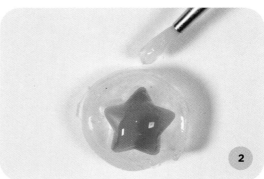

Doming with Resin

Doming is a finishing technique that adds an extra layer of resin to a surface of a piece to give a nice, bubble-like dome. I like to apply this technique to most of my flat resin pieces, to allow for a nicer finish. An optional step for most projects, pouring a new layer on top of a surface is also a great technique to cover up any undesirable resin surfaces, such as scratches, roughness, ripples, and other inconsistencies. You can use either UV resin or two-part resin for doming.

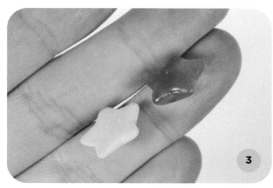

1. Place your piece flat side up on a silicone mat. Apply the resin into the middle of the piece.

2. With a silicone tool, toothpick, or basically anything pointed, spread the resin to the entire surface of the piece. Be careful when spreading the resin near the perimeters—the inevitable drips down the sides make it difficult to get an even finish.

3. Allow the resin to cure, either with time or under a UV light. The blue star is an unfinished flat piece, whereas the red star has a more bubbly, puffy look to it.

Working with Two-Part Resin

For those who have much more patience than I do or would like to tackle large-scale projects, using two-part, time-dependent resin is a great fit. One important advantage of two-part resin is that you don't need to have a UV light source, nor do you have to worry about making sure curing is consistent on all surfaces. If you mix the resin well, time will cure the piece without any hiccups. The main disadvantage is waiting twelve to twenty-four hours between each pour; most two-part resins usually take the full twenty-four hours to cure.

1. Measure out the recommended amount of each part of the resin into its own small, plastic container, as directed on the packaging. I like to use small sauce containers for measuring the resin, wiping away any excess with paper towel and cleaning the container with soap and water after each use.

2. Combine the two parts of resin in a third small container.

3. Slowly mix the combined resin with a popsicle stick, taking care to not trap air bubbles. The streaks in the photo are the two different parts of resin. Mix yours until any streaks disappear, which indicates a nicely mixed single compound.

4. Add any glitters and pigments you want. You don't have to be overly cautious while incorporating liquid pigments because two-part resin doesn't depend on light for curing. Fair warning, though: Adding too much liquid into resin will affect its chemical properties, making the resin quite sticky even if fully cured.

5. Pour the resin mixture into a mold.

6. Allow the resin to fully cure for twenty-four hours or as directed by the product instructions. After the piece is fully hardened, remove it from the mold.

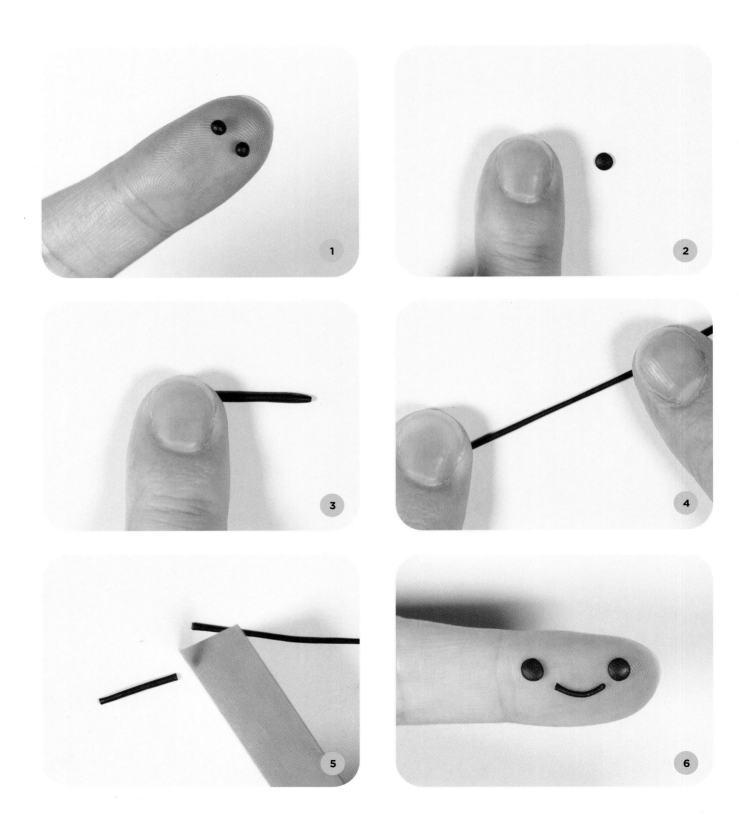

While this is an optional technique, I enjoy giving faces to many of my pieces, just to give them a bit of

Making a Polymer Clay Face

personality. Here I show you how to make eyes and a mouth out of polymer clay before adding it to your pieces.

1. Make two balls of black clay.

2. Flatten out the balls with your fingers to make two small, flat pancakes. Set these aside.

3. Roll out a piece of black clay under your finger.

4. Roll a thin snake of clay by holding one end while pulling and rolling the other end.

5. Cut the snake to the appropriate length. Curve it into a smile or frown, or keep it a straight line for a neutral look.

6. Bake the face. If I attach the face to my project before I bake any of it, I can bake the whole piece at once, then add resin. If I'm adding the face on top of resin, I bake the face pieces on their own before gluing them down.

Polymer Clay Basics

• Clean hands and a clean surface are important, especially when working with lighter colors, as any dirt, dust, and residue will easily transfer to the clay.
• If the clay is too dry, add a tiny bit of baby oil or condition it by kneading it continuously. If the clay is too soft, roll it flat and place it between two pieces of paper to absorb the oils in the clay and dry it out a bit.
• The clay shapes in my projects are very simple: spheres, pancakes, snakes, cylinders, or teardrops. Mastering these shapes allows you to focus on the proportions of each individual piece—which can be the hardest part of any project—and how you'll embellish it in your own way. If an element in a piece looks a bit strange, try making it bigger, smaller, wider, thinner, shorter, or longer.

Kawaii to Wear, Decorate, and Give

It's easy to make your kawaii resin and clay creations wearable or functional.
• Attach magnets, paperclips, or other metal embellishments or findings to make gifts and decorations.
• Incorporate an eye screw into your polymer clay project before baking it, then use a keyring, chains, or jewelry findings to make it wearable.
• Add an eye screw to resin pieces by making a small hole in the cured resin with a small, manual hand drill (sold at craft stores and online). Apply super glue to the thread end of the eye screw and insert it into the hole.

2

Kawaii
Nature
Tutorials

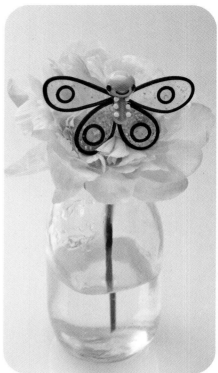

Butterfly

This butterfly is made using a stained-glass technique incorporating polymer clay outlines and mixtures of UV resin and glitter to create the wings. It's a fun project because you can easily change the design by adding more details and embellishments to the wings.

Supplies
- Polymer clay in pink, light blue, and black
- Polymer clay blade
- Clear packing tape
- UV or two-part resin
- Pigments
- Assorted glitters
- UV lamp (for UV resin or glaze, if used)
- Silicone mat
- Doming resin
- Super glue

Make the Butterfly's Head and Body

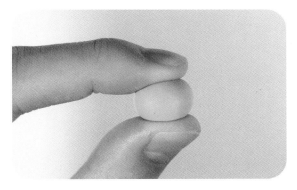

1. To make the head, slightly flatten out a ball of clay to make the shape of a nice plump dinner roll.

2. To make the body, take another ball of clay the same color as the head and roll it more on one side so the body is wider on one end.

3. Use a polymer clay blade to cut away the thinner end of the body. Keep the wider end to attach to the head.

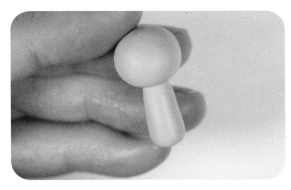

4. Attach the head to the cut end of the body. If the body seems too fat, thin, short, or long, re-roll the clay until you have perfect proportions.

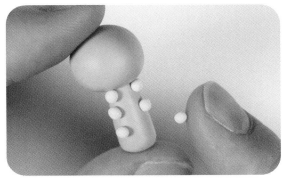

5. For the butterfly's legs, make six little balls of clay using a different color than the body. Attach them to the body, three on each side.

6. Use black clay to add two eyes and a mouth to the head.

Make and Glue on the Wings & Finish the Butterfly

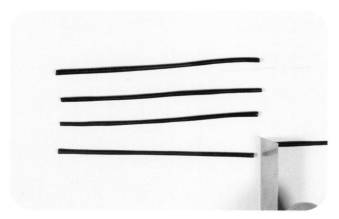

1. Roll out a thin snake of black clay. Cut it into four equal segments. Each segment will make up a section of a wing.

2. Shape a segment into a rounded scalene triangle for the top half of the wing. For the bottom half, shape a segment into a teardrop. Make two of each wing segment. To finish each segment, pinch the ends of the snake together.

3. Roll an additional snake of black clay to make four small rings. Bake the wings, the rings, and the body in the oven according to the manufacturer's instructions.

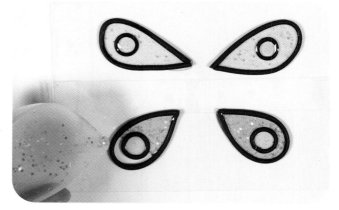

4. Place pieces of packing tape sticky side up on a flat work surface. Put the cured wing segments onto the tape, then put a ring within each segment. Make sure everything adheres completely. Pour resin mixtures of different colors into each wing and ring. I mixed colored resin with assorted glitters. Let your creativity roam free and make the design your own by using a variety of colors and embellishments.

5. After filling the wings, let the pieces cure. After curing, remove the tape from the backs of the wings.

6. To complete the wings, place them on a silicone mat, dome both sides with resin, and let them cure.

7. Apply super glue to one side of a segment where the ends of the snake meet. Place the segment on the back of the butterfly and apply pressure until the glue sets and the segment is firmly attached to the body. Repeat for the other three wing segments.

8. Once the glue is completely dry, apply a layer of glaze to the butterfly's body. Cure completely.

Weather Clouds

I made this series of clouds using a resin and polymer clay template as well as clay details. You'll create three different types of clouds: a cloud with a rainbow, a storm cloud, and a rain cloud.

Supplies

- Scrap polymer clay
- Supplies needed to make a silicone mold (see page 14)
- Polymer clay in yellow, light blue, red, orange, green, blue, and purple
- Black polymer clay for face (optional)
- Polymer clay blade
- UV or two-part resin
- Opaque white, opaque gray, and opaque light blue pigments
- UV lamp (for UV resin or glaze, if used)
- Super glue

Make the Cloud Template

1. Roll four balls of clay of different sizes. Flatten the balls into smooth dome shapes and place them next to each other.

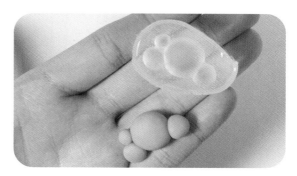

2. Bake the clay template in the oven according to the manufacturer's instructions, then make a silicone mold from it.

Make the Cloud Details

1. Next, work on the little clay details for the different clouds. Roll out a piece of yellow clay to make the lightning pieces.

2. Use a polymer clay blade to cut the yellow clay into lightning-bolt shapes.

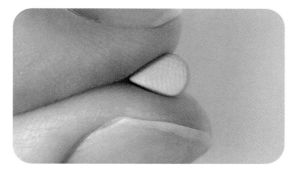

3. To make the raindrops, roll light blue clay into balls and pinch them into teardrop shapes.

4. Flatten the teardrop shapes.

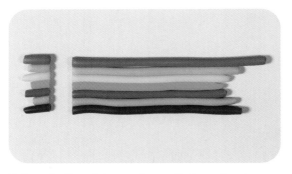

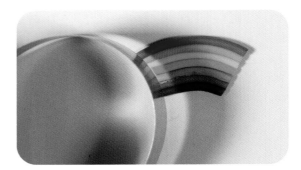

5. To make the rainbow, roll a small piece of each clay color into a snake. Align them together in the correct rainbow order (red, orange, yellow, green, blue, light blue, and purple). Trim one end straight with your blade.

6. Gently bend the rainbow into a curve, then flex the blade to cut the other end of the rainbow into a curve; this curve will eventually be glued to the cloud. Bake all the clay cloud details according to the manufacturer's instructions.

Make the Clouds & Add the Details

1. Create three different resin mixtures for the three different clouds: one opaque white, one opaque gray, and one opaque light blue.

2. Pour one of the mixtures into the mold and cure completely.

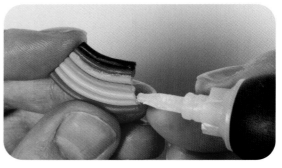

3. Repeat with the two other mixtures to create three different kinds of clouds.

4. Once all the clay pieces are fully baked and cooled, apply super glue to the curved part of the rainbow.

5. Press the rainbow onto the opaque white resin cloud.

6. Use super glue to adhere two lightning bolts onto the opaque gray resin cloud.

7. Glue the raindrops onto the opaque light blue resin cloud.

8. Your three clouds with glued polymer clay pieces are now complete. If you'd like to embellish them further, you can super glue on polymer clay face pieces and glaze the clouds with resin.

Flower

To create this cute little flower, in perfect bloom for the springtime, you'll make a polymer clay template along with clay details and a resin base.

Supplies

- Scrap polymer clay
- Supplies needed to make a silicone mold (see page 14)
- Polymer clay in light and dark green
- Polymer clay blade
- Black polymer clay for face (optional)
- UV or two-part resin
- Transparent pink pigment
- UV lamp (for UV resin or glaze, if used)
- Super glue
- Paintbrush or plastic stick

Make the Flower Template

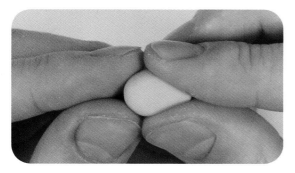

1. Pinch three pieces of scrap clay into large, medium, and small three-dimensional teardrop shapes.

2. Bake the pieces according to the manufacturer's instructions, let them cool, and then use them to make silicone molds (see page 14).

Make the Stem & the Leaves

1. To make the base of the flower, start by taking a ball of light green clay and flattening it into a pancake.

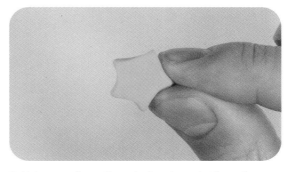

2. Using two fingertips, pinch out a point from the flattened pancake. Continue to rotate the pancake and pinch out sides until you have five points, which makes it resemble a star.

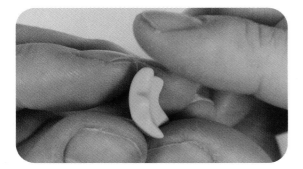

3. Smooth out the edges of the star shape with a finger and lightly bend down the points of the star to make it curved. The flower petals will sit upon this star base.

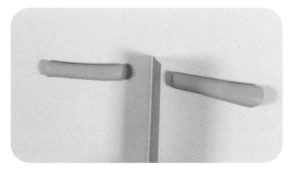

4. Roll out a thick snake of light green clay and cut off the ends to make the stem.

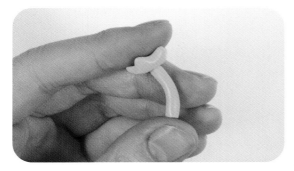

5. Slightly bend the stem and attach it to the convex side of the star.

6. Shape a flat piece of dark green clay into a teardrop, then pinch each end to make a diamond shape.

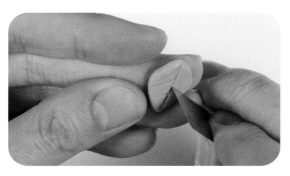

7. Use a polymer clay blade to make indents in the clay, creating a leaf pattern.

8. Repeat to make a second leaf.

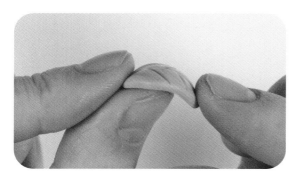

9. Gently bend the leaves so they curve slightly.

10. Attach the leaves to the stem. Make face pieces with the black clay (see page 23). Bake all pieces according to the manufacturer's instructions. Allow to cool.

Make the Petals & Finish the Flower

1. While the clay piece is baking, make a mixture of resin and transparent pink pigment and pour it into the silicone petal molds. Make one large petal and two each of the medium and small petals. Cure completely.

2. Remove the petals from the molds.

3. Glue the petals together with the largest one in the middle, the medium in back, and the smallest in front.

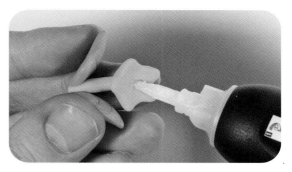

4. Once the stem and leaves have baked and cooled, place some super glue into the crater of the star.

5. Place the resin petals into the glue on the stem.

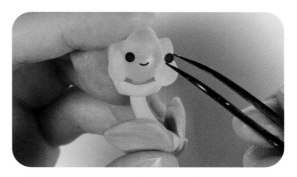

6. Glue the face onto the flower petals. Use a paintbrush to glaze the piece with resin. Cure completely.

Pine Tree

A wonderful symbol of wintertime, this little pine tree is topped with a shining star. This project is perfect for the winter holidays, as other decorations can be added for a festive tree.

Supplies

- Scrap polymer clay
- Supplies needed to make a silicone mold (see page 14)
- Polymer clay in dark brown, black, and yellow
- Polymer clay blade
- UV or two-part resin
- Green pigment
- UV lamp (for UV resin or glaze, if used)
- Super glue
- Paintbrush or plastic stick

Make the Tree Template

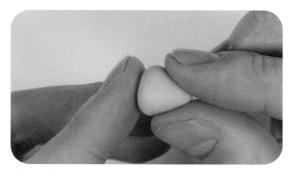

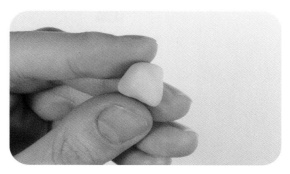

1. To make the template for the leaves of the pine tree, pinch some scrap clay into a pyramid shape with a triangle base. Think of it as a four-sided die.

2. Pinch out the corners of the pyramid to make it a bit longer and rounded. This will be the top of the tree.

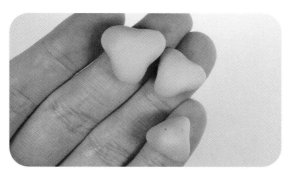

3. Repeat to make the bottom two tiers of the tree. The top part of the tree should be the smallest, with each tier beneath it slightly bigger.

4. Stack the three tiers on top of each other. Bake the clay template according to the manufacturer's instructions, let it cool and then use it to make a silicone mold (see page 14).

Make the Trunk & the Star

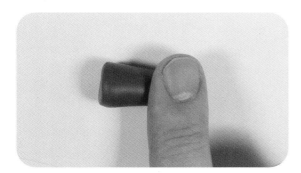

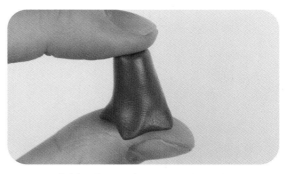

1. To make the trunk, roll dark brown clay into a thick cylinder.

2. As you did for the tree leaves, pinch out the roots of the trunk with two fingers and round them out.

3. Cut off excess clay with a polymer clay blade.

4. Use black clay to make a face (see page 23), and add it to the tree trunk for extra cuteness.

5. To make a star for the top of the tree, flatten some yellow clay into a thick pancake shape.

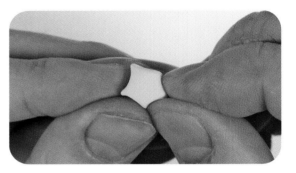

6. With the same pinching technique you used for the tree tiers and the roots of the trunk, pinch out five points in the yellow clay for the star.

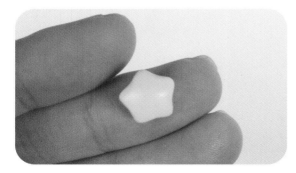

7. After rounding off the ends and smoothing the edges with your finger, the final product should be a chubby star.

8. To make the star even cuter, use black clay to make a face. Bake the clay trunk and star according to the manufacturer's instructions, then cool.

Finish the Tree

1. Mix green pigment into resin. Pour the mixture into the silicone mold for the tree. Cure completely.

2. Carefully remove the tree from the mold.

3. Apply super glue to the bottom of the resin tree and attach the trunk to it.

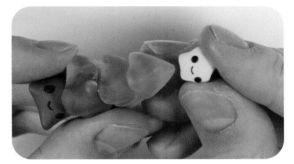

4. Glue the star to the tip of the tree, making sure the faces on the trunk and the star are facing in the same direction. To finish the tree, brush on a layer of resin for extra shine. Cure completely.

Snowman

Another winter seasonal staple is an adorable little snowman. I made a very simplified snowman, but you can customize it to your liking by adding a scarf, a different face, or other clothing materials.

Supplies
- Polymer clay in brown, orange, and black
- Supplies needed to make a silicone mold (see page 14)
- Polymer clay blade
- UV or two-part resin
- Opaque white pigment
- UV lamp (for UV resin or glaze, if used)
- Super glue
- Paintbrush or plastic stick

Make the Snowman Template

To make the clay template, roll two balls of clay, one a little bit smaller than the other. After curing the clay in the oven according to the manufacturer's instructions, use the pieces to make a silicone mold. I made the template as two separate balls; however, you may choose to assemble them, bake the snowman as one piece, and then make a single mold.

Make the Snowman's Features

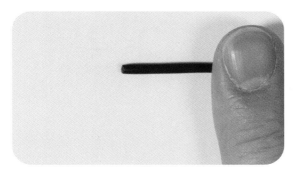

1. Start by making the stick arms for the snowman. Roll out some brown clay into a thick snake.

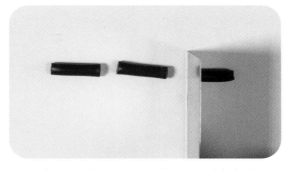

2. Cut the snake into two equal lengths with a polymer clay blade to make the main branches of the arms.

3. For the little branches, roll a slightly thinner snake of brown clay and cut the clay at an angle.

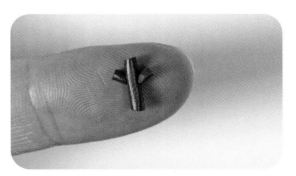

4. Assemble the branch pieces.

5. For the little carrot nose, roll a cylinder of orange clay, making one side super pointy, and cut off the end.

6. To give the snowman a hat, flatten out black clay into a thin pancake shape and cut out a small notch. I was inspired to give my snowman the old ripped-up hat from my memories of cartoon snowmen.

7. For the top part of the hat, roll out a thick cylinder of black clay and cut off the excess.

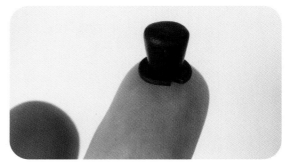

8. Assemble the hat pieces. Once fully assembled, bake all the clay details in the oven according to the manufacturer's instructions. I also added a few extra flattened dots of black clay for the buttons and eyes, and a thin snake for a smile.

Finish the Snowman

1. Carefully mix opaque white pigment with the resin and pour it into the silicone molds. Cure completely.

2. Attach the two parts of the snowman's body (unless you created the entire body as one mold). I attached the snowman body parts with UV resin, but super glue works just as well.

3. Once the snowman is assembled, you can add the little clay details. Start by adding the face with super glue.

4. Add the little dots on the body for buttons.

5. Glue the top hat to the snowman's head at a slight slant to give it character.

6. Add the branch arms using super glue. Once all the snowman's little features have been added, give it a nice layer of glaze and cure completely.

Kawaii

Marine Life

Tutorials

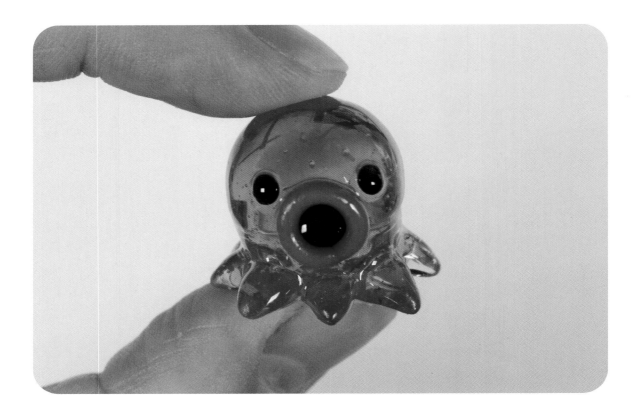

Octopus

Let's go into the ocean and pick out a cute little octopus from the depths. You will learn how to make this little octopus using a polymer clay template, clay details, and a resin base.

Supplies
- Scrap polymer clay
- Polymer clay blade
- Supplies needed to make a silicone mold (see page 14)
- UV or two-part resin
- Red pigment
- UV lamp (for UV resin or glaze, if used)
- Super glue
- Polymer clay in black and red
- Paintbrush or plastic stick

Make the Octopus Template

1. Roll a piece of scrap clay into a ball for the body.

2. Roll a piece of clay into a snake, tapering one end into a soft point. Trim the excess with a polymer clay blade.

3. Because it's an octopus, I made eight arms this way, but it's totally okay to settle for fewer arms if you can't fit them all.

4. Add one arm to the body at a time, until all eight of them are attached.

5. Cut your template in two. It may seem strange, but this allows for a smoother surface overall. You can keep it in one piece, but it will be trickier to make.

6. After baking the template according to the manufacturer's instructions, let it cool, and use it to make a silicone mold.

Make the Resin Piece & Add the Details

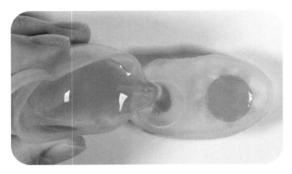

1. Mix red pigment into resin and pour it into the mold. Cure completely.

2. Once the resin is cured, pop the resin pieces out of the mold.

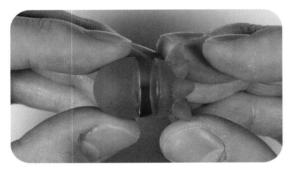

3. Apply super glue to one half of the body and press the two halves together.

4. To make the octopus mouth, flatten out black clay into a pancake shape.

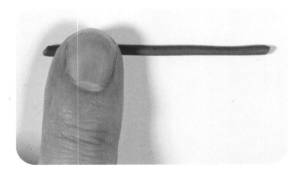

5. Roll some red clay into a thick snake.

6. Wrap the red clay snake around the black circle. Cut away the excess red clay and then blend the two ends of the snake together. Once you complete the mouth, make two eyes from black clay. Bake the clay pieces according to the manufacturer's instructions. Let cool.

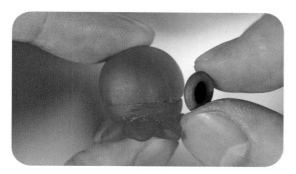

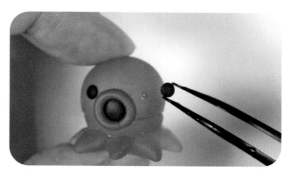

7. Once the clay has cooled, super glue the mouth in the center of the octopus.

8. Glue on the eyes. Apply a layer of resin for glaze. Cure completely, and the octopus is finished!

Snails

For this tutorial, you'll make three snails, each with a different shell. The shells are made of resin and the rest is all made from clay.

Supplies

- Scrap polymer clay
- Supplies needed to make a silicone mold (see page 14)
- Pink, magenta, purple, and glitter pigments
- UV or two-part resin
- UV lamp (for UV resin or glaze, if used)
- Polymer clay in pearl and black
- Super glue
- Paintbrush or plastic stick

Make the Shell Template

1. To make the first shell, roll some scrap clay into a snake, making sure to roll more on one end to make it into a point.

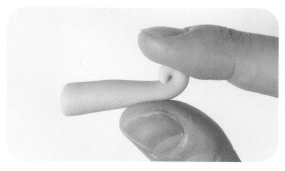

2. Starting at the pointed end, carefully roll the snake into a lollipop swirl.

3. Complete the lollipop swirl.

4. To make the second shell, twist another pointed clay snake, starting at the wider end.

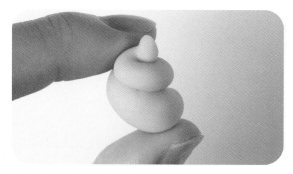

5. Continue to gently twist the snake to create a swirl that looks like a soft-serve ice cream.

6. To make the third shell, slightly flatten a ball of clay on one side. Add a small ball of clay, flattening it onto the main shell.

7. Add a smaller ball of clay on top of the second layer.

8. Once all three shells are made, bake them according to the manufacturer's instructions. Let them cool, and then make silicone molds.

Make the Resin Pieces & Complete Each Snail

1. For each shell, mix your pigments into resin. I used different pigments of pink, magenta, and purple, with glitters added for extra detail.

2. Pour each mixture into its mold, and cure completely.

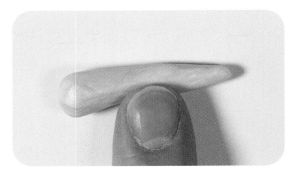

3. To make the first snail's body, roll pearl clay into a snake. Roll more on one side, so one side is thicker than the other.

4. Bend the thicker end at a slight slant upward, making sure it follows the curve of the lollipop swirl shell.

5. Add a couple of eyes and a smile (see page 23).

6. Bake the body according to the manufacturer's instructions, and let it cool. Apply super glue to the top of the body and place the lollipop swirl shell onto it.

7. Add a layer of glaze, cure completely, and the first snail is ready!

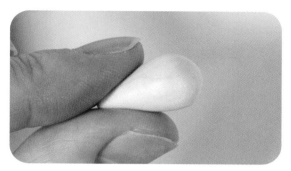

8. For the second snail, pinch more pearl clay into a teardrop shape.

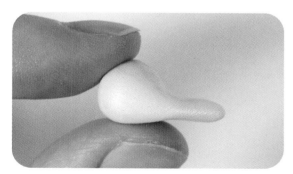

9. Squish the skinny part of the teardrop flat between two fingers.

10. Add a face to the body, and bake according to the manufacturer's instructions. Allow it to cool, and then glue the body onto the shell made by flattened balls stacked atop one another.

11. Finish the second snail with a layer of glaze. Cure completely.

12. For the third snail, repeat the teardrop shape, flattening it for the body.

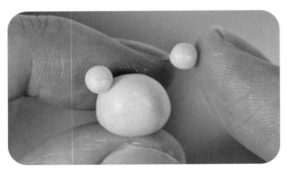

13. For the eyes, place two small balls of pearly clay on the head part of the snail.

14. Place little dots of black clay on the pearly eyes, and add a smile.

15. Bake the body according to the manufacturer's instructions. Allow it to cool.

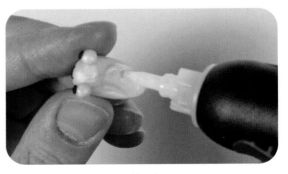

16. Apply glue to the snail body.

17. Press the body against the shell resembling soft-serve ice cream.

18. Add a layer of glaze and cure completely to complete this snail.

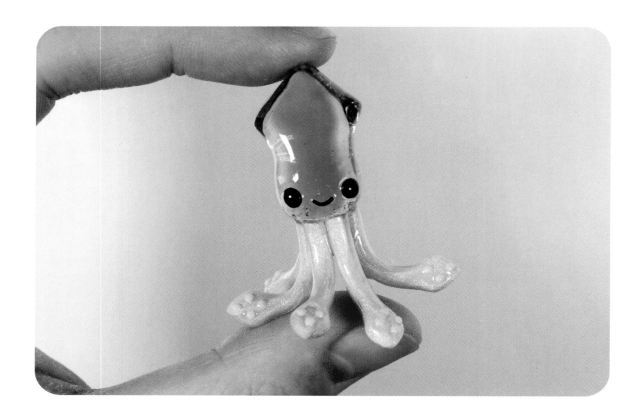

Squid

The body of this six-armed squid is made of resin using a polymer clay template, and the arms are made of clay.

Supplies
- Scrap polymer clay
- Supplies needed to make a silicone mold (see page 14)
- Polymer clay in pearl, mint, and black
- UV or two-part resin
- Blue pigment
- UV lamp (for UV resin or glaze, if used)
- Super glue
- Paintbrush or plastic stick

Make the Squid Template

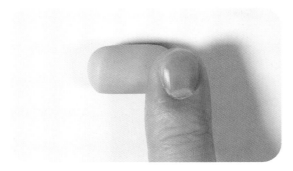

1. Roll scrap clay into a thick cylinder shape.

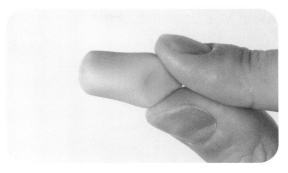

2. Pinch one end of the cylinder into a point.

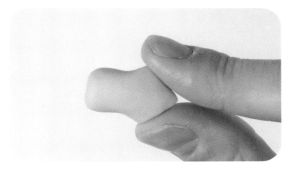

3. Pinch part of the point outward, to make it more into an arrow shape.

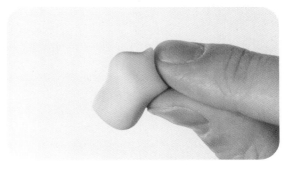

4. Pinch the front and back sides to shape it into a diamond (when viewed from the top).

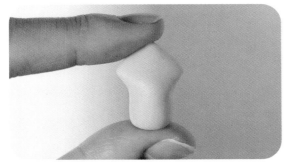

5. Bake the completed template according to the manufacturer's instructions. Let it cool.

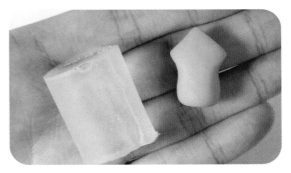

6. Use the template to create a silicone mold.

Make the Clay Arms & Face

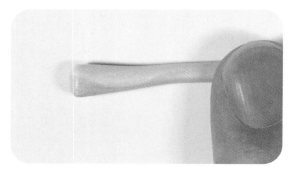

1. To make the clay arms, roll pearl clay into a thick snake, leaving one end of the cylinder slightly thicker.

2. Press the thicker end flat with a finger.

3. The resulting shape will look sort of like a spoon.

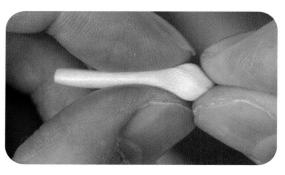

4. Pinch the flattened end into a diamond shape. Make five more arms for a total of six.

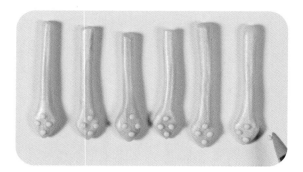

5. Place four individual dots of mint clay on the diamond portions of the arms.

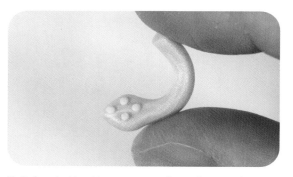

6. Before baking the arms as well as a face made out of clay (see page 23), bend all six arms in different directions so the squid can stand. Feel free to pose your squid's arms in various ways, making it your own. Bake the clay pieces, then let them cool.

Make the Resin Base & Finish the Squid

1. Make a mixture of blue pigment and resin. Pour it into the silicone mold and cure completely.

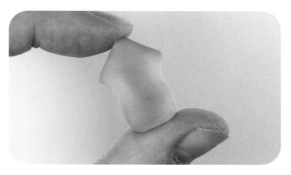

2. Carefully remove the body from the mold.

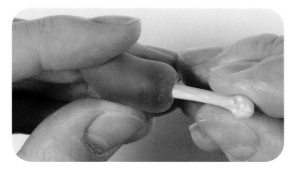

3. Place super glue onto the bottom of the squid body, then attach one clay arm at a time.

4. Continue attaching each arm until all six are connected. Once all the arms are attached, add the face. For the final touch, brush on a layer of resin glaze to add shine. Cure completely.

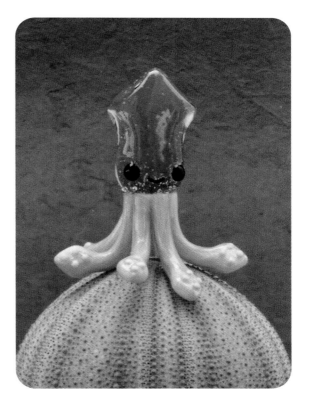

Jellyfish

This project shows how to make three different varieties of jellyfish. Customize your pieces by using your own designs on top and different tentacles.

Supplies

- Scrap polymer clay
- Supplies needed to make a silicone mold (see page 14)
- UV or two-part resin
- Opaque pastel pigments
- UV lamp (for UV resin or glaze, if used)
- Polymer clay in translucent and black
- Polymer clay blade
- Clay roller
- Super glue
- Paintbrush or plastic stick

Make the Jellyfish Template & Mold the Resin

1. The template for the jellyfish is very simple. Slightly squish a ball of clay between two fingers.

2. From the top, the template should look like a circle; from the side, it should look like an oval.

3. Bake the template according to the manufacturer's instructions and allow to cool. Then use it to make a silicone mold.

4. Mix small amounts of opaque pastel pigments into resin. Pour this mixture into the silicone mold, and cure completely.

Make the Clay Tentacles

1. For the first type of tentacle, roll out some translucent clay into a snake, making one side a bit thicker than the other. It should look like a really long teardrop shape.

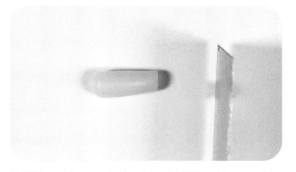

2. With a polymer clay blade, cut off the skinny end.

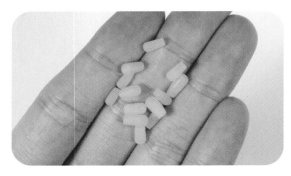

3. Make a bunch of these tentacles. You can never have too many.

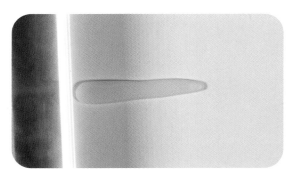

4. For the second type of tentacle, roll out another thin snake of translucent clay. Using a clay roller, flatten out the clay.

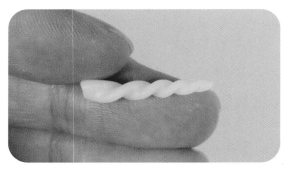

5. Next, twist the piece of clay, giving it a spiral appearance.

6. Once again, make a bunch of these tentacles, all of different lengths. Bake the tentacles, as well as optional facial features (see page 23), according to the manufacturer's instructions. Allow to cool.

Finish the Jellyfish

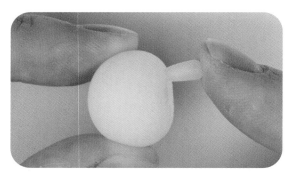

1. Apply super glue to some stubby tentacles and attach them in a circle to the bottom of the first jellyfish, close to the side.

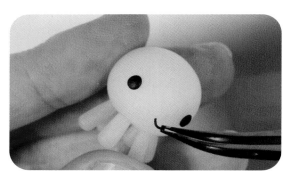

2. Give the jellyfish a cute little face as well.

3. For the second type of jellyfish, glue the spiral tentacles to the center of the jellyfish head.

4. Bunch all the tentacles together.

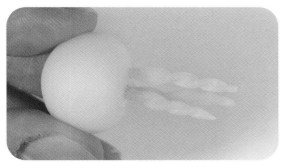

5. For the third jellyfish, combine the two previous jellyfish designs. Add the spiral tentacles in the center.

6. Place the stubby tentacles in a circle along the sides of the jellyfish. Once you've made all three types of jellyfish, including optional faces, give them a layer of resin glaze. It's easy to customize this project with more or fewer tentacles, different shapes, and even a nice design on the head.

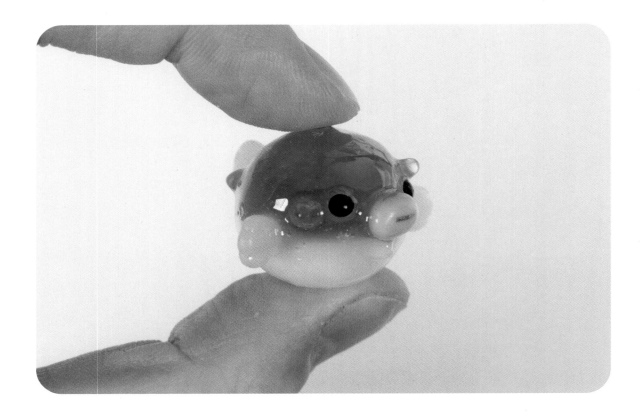

Pufferfish

The last marine creature on the list is a pufferfish. This little guy is known for ballooning up when he's in a panic. You'll use a polymer clay template to make a resin base, adding clay details.

Supplies

- Scrap polymer clay
- Polymer clay blade
- Supplies needed to make a silicone mold (see page 14)
- UV or two-part resin
- Blue and opaque white pigments
- UV lamp (for UV resin or glaze, if used)
- Polymer clay in translucent white, pink, and black
- Super glue
- Paintbrush or plastic stick

Make the Pufferfish Template

1. Use a ball of scrap clay for the body. This ball should be slightly larger than those used for previous templates.

2. Roll clay into a tapered snake. With a polymer clay blade, cut off just the little point. Repeat until you have enough spikes for your pufferfish.

3. Place the spikes all around the body, making sure there's enough space between them to add a face and the rest of the details (two side fins and a tail).

4. Once completed, bake the template according to the manufacturer's instructions. Let the clay cool, and then use it to make a silicone mold.

Make the Resin Base

1. Add blue pigment to resin.

2. Pour the mixture into the silicone mold about two-thirds full. Let it cure.

3. Make an opaque white pigment resin mixture. Pour it into the remaining third of the mold, and let that cure as well.

4. Once the pufferfish body is fully cured, carefully take it out of the mold.

Make the Clay Details & Finish the Pufferfish

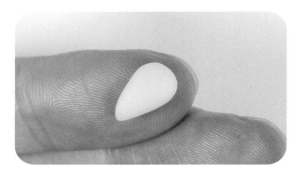

1. To make the fin, roll some translucent white clay into a teardrop shape, then flatten it out with your fingers.

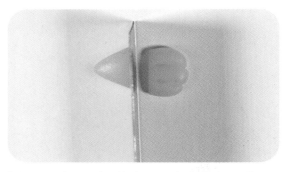

2. Use a polymer clay blade to make indents on the wide end of the teardrop to give it that extra fin-like design. With the blade, cut off the narrow end of the teardrop. I made two of them for the side fins.

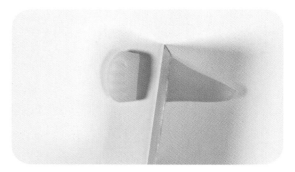

3. Using a larger piece of clay, repeat steps 1 and 2 to make a tail fin.

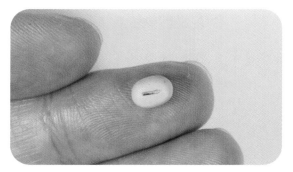

4. Make the pufferfish's mouth by flattening some pink clay into an oval shape. Using the tip of the polymer clay blade, make an indent in the middle.

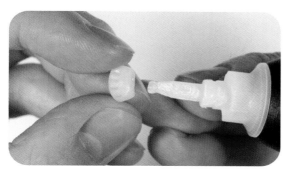

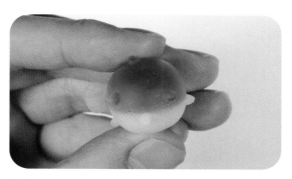

5. Once you make all the clay pieces, including a pair of eyes, bake them according to the manufacturer's instructions, allowing ample time for them to cool. Then apply super glue to the edge of the tail fin.

6. Place the tail fin on the pufferfish, making sure it's oriented perpendicular to the blue–white resin color division.

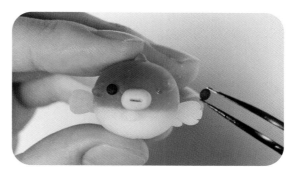

7. Glue the smaller fins on each side of the pufferfish.

8. Between the side fins, and on the opposite side from the tail, glue the mouth onto the body. Add the eyes. Brush on a layer of resin glaze for extra glimmer. Cure completely.

4

Kawaii
Animal
Tutorials

Pig

Having mastered marine life, you'll now learn how to make land animals. The first project in this category, this cute little pig has a resin body with polymer clay details.

Supplies

- Scrap polymer clay
- Supplies needed to make a silicone mold (see page 14)
- UV or two-part resin
- Pink pigment
- UV lamp (for UV resin or glaze, if used)
- Polymer clay in light pink, dark pink, and black
- Polymer clay blade
- Super glue
- Paintbrush or plastic stick

Make the Template & Resin Mold for the Pig's Body

1. Roll one a ball of clay on one axis to elongate it slightly. Gently press the resulting cylinder to make a uniform oval.

2. Bake the template according to the manufacturer's instructions, let it cool, and then make a silicone mold out of it.

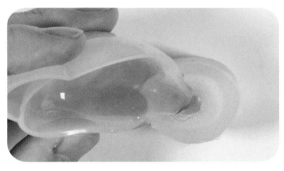

3. Make a mixture of pink pigment and resin and pour it into the silicone mold. Cure completely.

4. Carefully remove the pig's body from the mold.

Make the Pig Details

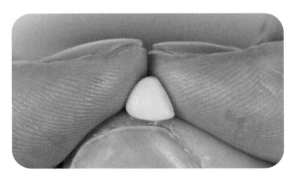

1. To make the pig's ears, pinch a flat circle of light pink clay into a flat triangle.

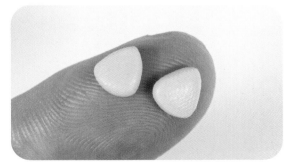

2. Make two of them.

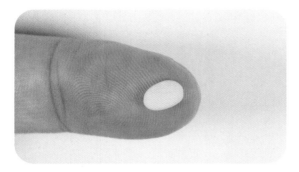

3. For the pig's snout, roll the same light pink clay into an oval shape and flatten it.

4. Add darker pink dots of clay onto the light pink oval for the nostrils.

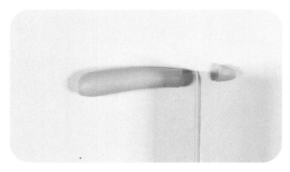

5. For the pig's little feet, roll the light pink clay into a snake, rolling more on one side to make it pointy. Use a polymer clay blade to cut off the pointed end.

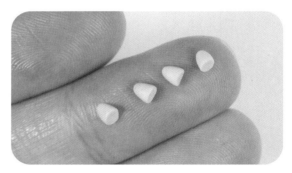

6. Repeat the process until you have four feet in total.

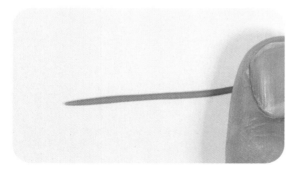

7. For the pig's tail, roll dark pink clay into a thin snake.

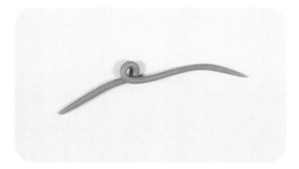

8. Gently lift one end of the snake and create a loop for a curly tail.

9. Repeat to finish curling the tail. Trim the rough ends.

10. Make facial features out of black clay (see page 23), and then bake all the clay details according to the manufacturer's instructions. Allow to cool.

Finish the Pig

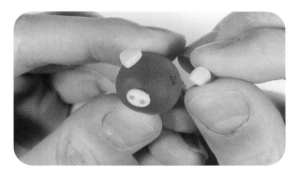

1. Apply super glue to the resin body of the pig. Glue on the ears and snout.

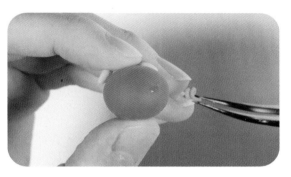

2. Glue the swirly tail on the end of the body opposite the ears and snout.

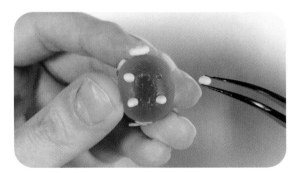

3. Add the little feet.

4. Don't forget the face. Brush on a layer of glaze, cure completely, and the pig is done.

Chicken & Chick

This project shows how to make a cute little chicken, as well as an adorable little chick. Both use the same clay template and mold, but with different polymer clay details.

Supplies
- Scrap polymer clay
- Supplies needed to make a silicone mold (see page 14)
- Pearl pigment
- UV or two-part resin
- Yellow pigment
- UV lamp (for UV resin or glaze, if used)
- Polymer clay in white, red, orange, and black
- Polymer clay blade
- Clay roller
- Paper for template
- Super glue
- Paintbrush or plastic stick

Make the Template, Mold, and Bodies

1. Pinch and roll a ball of clay into a chubby egg shape.

2. Bake the template according to the manufacturer's instructions, let it cool, and then make a silicone mold out of it.

3. For the chicken's body, make a mixture of pearl pigment and resin, and pour it into the silicone mold. Let it cure completely before removing it from the mold.

4. For the chick, make a yellow pigment resin mixture and pour it into the mold. Allow it to cure completely before removing it from the mold.

Make the Chicken & Chick Details

1. For the chicken's tail, roll out three different lengths of white clay into snakes. Align them next to each other and pinch the ends together.

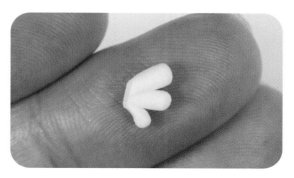

2. Use a polymer clay blade to cut off the excess clay along the bottom of the tail feathers, where they all meet.

3. Next, make the head feathers for a chicken or the comb as on a rooster. Roll out some red clay with a roller.

4. Cut out a simple paper template of an uneven heart shape. Trace out the template on the red clay, and then cut it out with a polymer clay blade. Smooth the edges with a finger.

5. Press the comb against the already cured resin body to give it a curved shape.

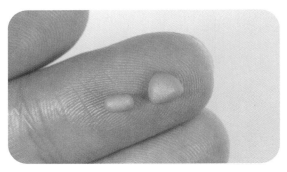

6. For the chicken's beak, pinch orange clay into a triangular pyramid shape with rounded corners. For the chick's beak, roll some orange clay into an oval shape.

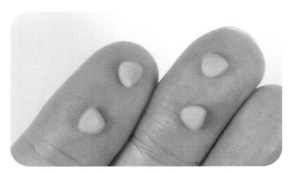

7. For the feet of both chicken and chick, pinch more orange clay into four flat triangles.

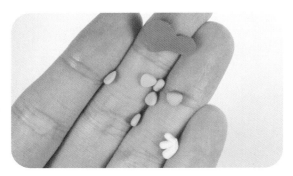

8. Bake all the clay pieces, including four small black eyes, according to the manufacturer's instructions. (Because the chicken and chick have beaks, no mouths are needed.) Allow to cool.

Finish the Chicken & the Chick

1. Glue the comb to the head of the chicken. Since you curved the comb against the resin piece before baking, it should fit like a glove. Next, glue on the triangular beak, aligning it with and on the taller side of the comb.

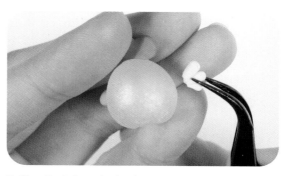

2. Glue the tail on the body opposite the beak.

3. Attach the triangle feet to the chicken, on the same side of the body as the beak but lower.

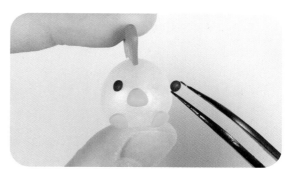

4. Glue on two eyes.

5. For the chick, glue on its oval beak and the two triangle feet.

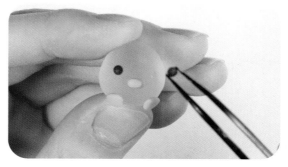

6. Add the eyes. To finish, brush a layer of glaze on both chicken and chick. Cure completely.

Panda

This project is a bit tricky because of the proportions, but the end result is very satisfying. It's a cute little panda, with three layers of resin and polymer clay details.

Supplies

- Scrap polymer clay
- Supplies needed to make a silicone mold (see page 14)
- UV or two-part resin
- Opaque white and black pigments
- UV lamp (for UV resin or glaze, if used)
- Polymer clay in black, pink, and white
- Dotting tool
- Polymer clay blade
- Super glue
- Paintbrush or plastic stick

Make the Panda Body

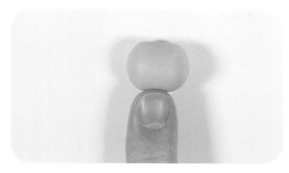

1. This template is one of the simplest in the book. Roll a ball of clay slightly on its side. It should look like a fat oval.

2. Bake the template according to the manufacturer's instructions, let it cool, and make a silicone mold out of it.

3. Make a mixture of opaque white pigment and resin for the first layer. Fill one third to one half of the mold with it. Cure completely.

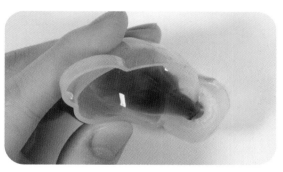

4. Mix black pigment and resin for the second layer. Fill about one fourth of the mold with it, on top of the first layer. Cure completely.

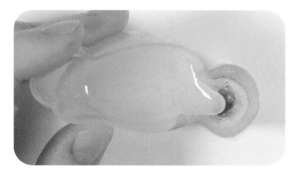

5. Finally, fill the rest of the mold with the same opaque white resin mixture used for the first layer. Cure that layer completely.

6. This is how the panda looks so far. It can be difficult to get the proportions of the resin layers right, so if it looks a bit off, you can always try it again. It took me a couple of tries to get a proportion I liked.

Make the Panda Details

1. Start by making the panda's ears. Roll out a black piece of clay into an oval shape and flatten it out with your fingers. Use a dotting tool to make an oval indent in the middle.

2. In that indent, place a pink oval piece of clay and use the dotting tool to smooth it out.

3. Split this in half with a polymer clay blade, and you have two ears, just like that.

4. For the feet, roll out black and white clay individually into snakes. Cut off the rounded ends to make two black feet and two white feet.

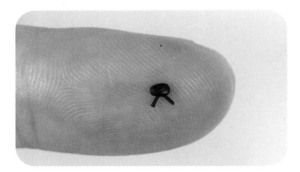

5. For the mouth and nose of the panda, roll out two extremely thin snakes of black clay and attach them to a flattened oval piece of black clay. Place the snakes under the wide side of the oval, in an inverted "V" formation.

6. For the eyes, stack a small dot of white clay on top of a flattened black pancake. Do this twice. Bake the completed clay details according to the manufacturer's instructions. Allow to cool.

Finish the Panda

1. Apply super glue to the ears and attach them to one of the white parts of the panda.

2. Next, glue on the two eyes, making sure the white pupils are facing each other toward the bottom.

3. Between the eyes, attach the mouth/nose piece.

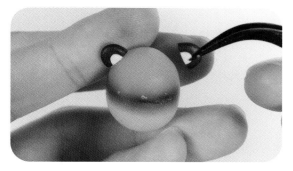

4. Attach the black feet to the bottom part of the panda, where the resin is white. Glue the white feet to the black part of the resin. Apply a layer of resin with a paintbrush, cure completely, and the cute little panda is done!

Penguin

Ever since I was a child, I thought penguins were one of the cutest creatures alive, so of course I had to include a penguin tutorial in this book. Like other projects, the penguin has a resin base and polymer clay details. You'll learn a different technique of baking polymer clay on pre-baked clay, which the steps in this project thoroughly explain.

Supplies
- Scrap polymer clay
- Polymer clay blade
- Supplies needed to make a silicone mold (see page 14)
- UV or two-part resin
- Black pigment
- UV lamp (for UV resin or glaze, if used)
- Polymer clay in white, orange, and black
- Clay roller
- Paper for a template
- Cornstarch (optional)
- Super glue
- Paintbrush or plastic stick

Make the Penguin Body

1. Roll a ball of clay to make a slightly chubby oval shape, very similar to the panda template (see page 81).

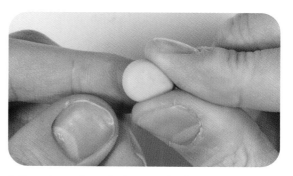

2. To make a wing, pinch some clay into a triangle shape.

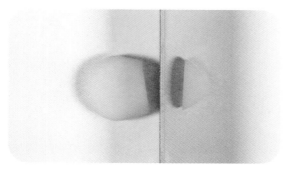

3. Using a polymer clay blade, cut the tip of the triangle at a slant.

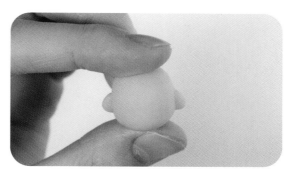

4. Repeat steps 2 and 3 to make a second wing. Place a wing on each side of the penguin.

5. Bake the template according to the manufacturer's instructions, let it cool, and then use it to make a silicone mold.

6. Pour a mixture of black pigment and resin into the silicone mold. Cure completely.

Make the Penguin Details

1. Begin with the penguin's face. The first step is to flatten white clay using a roller.

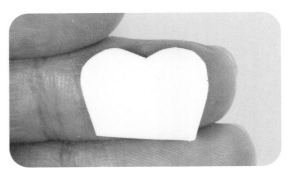

2. Make a paper template in the shape of a rounded M. With a polymer clay blade, cut out the white clay using the template as a guide. Smooth the edges.

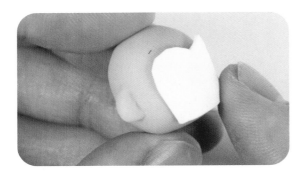

3. Press the face onto the baked penguin body template. Rather than blending the face on the template, just lightly press it, which should allow it to easily come off once baked. To make removal easier, rub a small amount of cornstarch on the template before pressing on the face. Cornstarch will help keep the clay from sticking while it's baking.

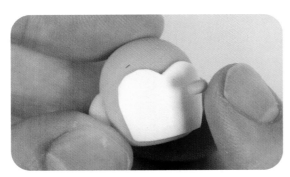

4. For the penguin beak, place a little orange oval, similar to the chick's beak on page 78, on the face where the arches meet.

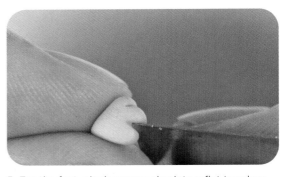

5. For the feet, pinch orange clay into a flat teardrop shape. Use your polymer clay blade to make two indents on the wide end of the teardrop shape.

6. Repeat the previous step so that you have two little feet.

7. Make two black dots for eyes and put them on the face. Then bake all the clay details in the oven according to the manufacturer's instructions. Allow them to cool.

Finish the Penguin

1. Once all the clay pieces are baked, slowly peel off the face from the template. Be very gentle to avoid cracking the face. I usually wedge my nails around the edges and carefully peel it off.

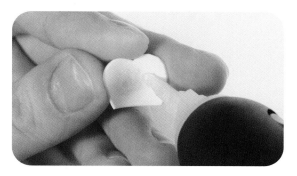

2. Apply super glue to the back of the penguin face.

3. Attach the face to the penguin's body.

4. Glue on the penguin's feet. To finish the penguin, brush on a layer of resin glaze. Cure completely.

Mouse

The final animal in this chapter is a cute little mouse (not a computer mouse, but the kind that squeaks!). You'll use two polymer clay templates to make a resin base and add polymer clay details to finish.

Supplies

- Scrap polymer clay
- Polymer clay blade
- Supplies needed to make a silicone mold (see page 14)
- UV or two-part resin
- Light purple pigment
- UV lamp (for UV resin or glaze, if used)
- Polymer clay in light blue, pink, and black
- Super glue
- Paintbrush or plastic stick

Make the Body & Ears

1. For the main body of the mouse, pinch scrap clay into a three-dimensional teardrop shape.

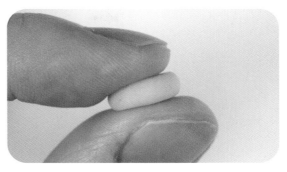

2. You'll also need a mold for the ears. Use your fingers to flatten out a ball of clay into a pancake shape.

3. Use a polymer clay blade to cut off a small end of the circle.

4. Bake the two templates according to the manufacturer's instructions, let them cool, and then make each template into a silicone mold.

5. Pour a mixture of light purple pigment and resin into the two molds. Cure completely before removing the pieces from the molds.

6. Pour a second resin ear. Cure completely before removing it from the mold.

Make the Mouse Details

1. Flatten two balls of light blue clay for the insides of the mouse's ears.

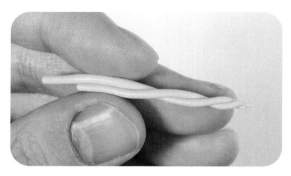

2. To make the tail, roll out two pink clay snakes of equal length and thickness. Align and press them together, then begin twisting them.

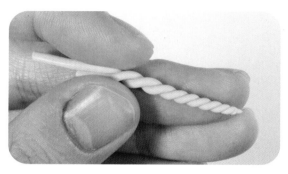

3. Continue twisting the two pieces of clay together until they are as long as you'd like.

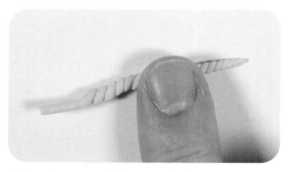

4. Use a finger to roll the twisted tail to make it smooth. Make sure to gently roll it to retain the lines in the tail.

5. Using a polymer clay blade, cut off the excess clay, then bend the tail so that it curves.

6. For the mouse's whiskers, roll out a thin snake of black clay and cut it into four equal lengths.

7. For the mouse's nose, make a small pink oval. Make two small black eyes.

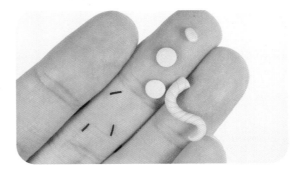

8. Bake all the clay pieces according to the manufacturer's instructions. Allow them to cool.

Finish the Mouse

1. Apply super glue to the resin ears and attach a light blue dot to each. Glue the ears to the mouse's body, with the light blue parts facing the pointy end.

2. Add the pink nose on the pointy end of the mouse's body.

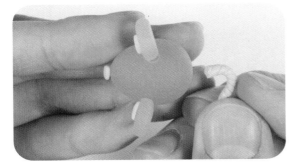

3. Attach the tail to the end of the body opposite the nose.

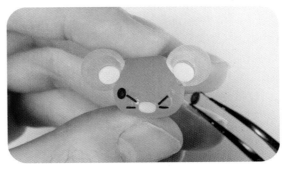

4. Glue the whiskers to the sides of the nose, two on each side. Glue on the eyes. Brush a resin glaze on your mouse for extra shine, cure completely, and you're done.

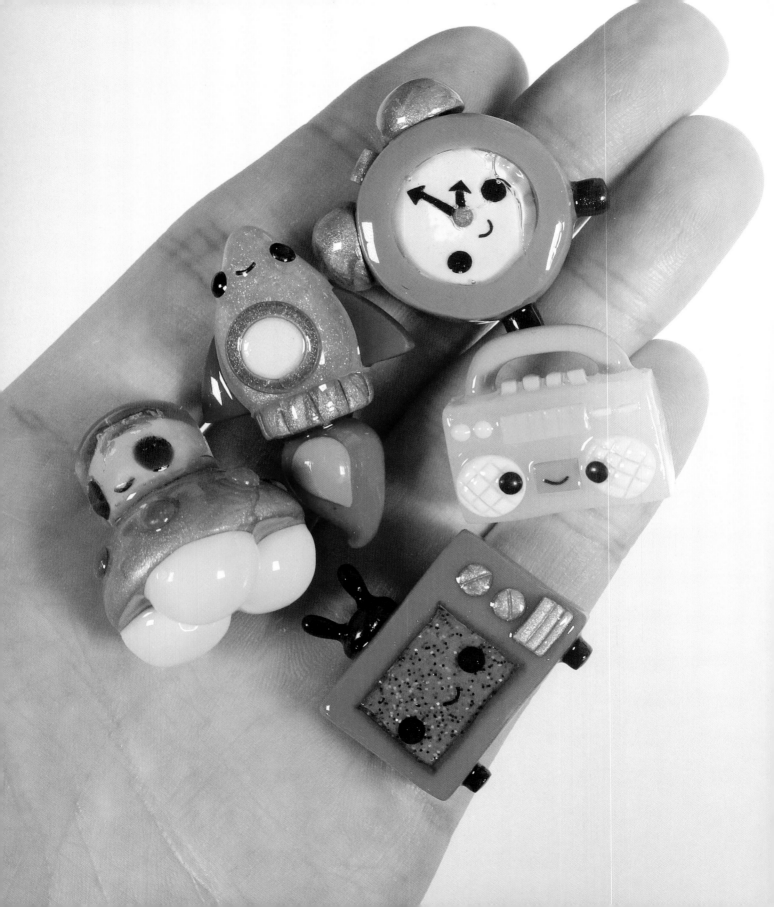

5

Kawaii Electronics & Objects Tutorials

Alarm Clock

The first tutorial in the electronics/objects category, this project uses both resin and polymer clay. Unlike most of the other projects, however, you don't need to make a mold.

Supplies

- Polymer clay in white, blue, gold, silver, and black
- Clay roller
- Polymer clay blade
- UV or two-part resin
- UV lamp (for UV resin or glaze, if using)
- Paintbrush or plastic stick

Make the Clock Face

1. Start the face of the clock with a ball of white clay.

2. Press the ball of white clay into a flat pancake shape.

3. For the frame around the clock's face, roll out a thick snake of blue clay, and then roll it flat with a clay roller. Make sure the strip of clay is thick. Using a polymer clay blade, cut the strip of clay into a rectangle.

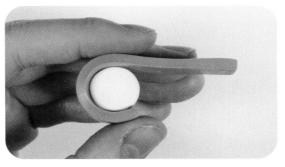

4. Wrap the rectangular strip around the clock's face.

5. Cut off the excess clay and blend the ends of the strip together.

6. Use black clay to add eyes and a mouth to the clock's face.

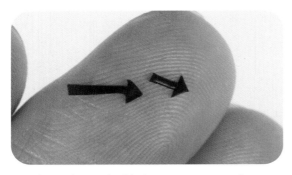

7. With a polymer clay blade, cut out two small arrows from a flattened piece of black clay, one shorter than the other.

8. Place the arrows on the face of the clock. I placed them at two o'clock, but you can change the time to whatever you like. Add a little gold dot of clay where the arrows meet, for a nose.

Finish the Clock

1. To make the alarm bells, start with a ball of silver clay. Use your blade to cut the silver ball in half.

2. Place the two halves on the top of the alarm clock.

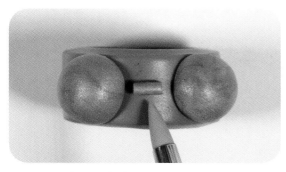

3. Between the two bell halves, place a little silver oval, which is the little hammer that hits the bells when the clock rings.

4. For the clock's feet, roll out black clay into a thick cylinder, and cut it into two small pieces.

5. Place the feet on the bottom of the clock. Bake the entire piece according to the manufacturer's instructions. Allow it to cool.

6. Carefully fill the clock's face with resin, so it has a domed look to it. Cure completely. To finish the clock, paint on a layer of resin glaze. Cure that completely.

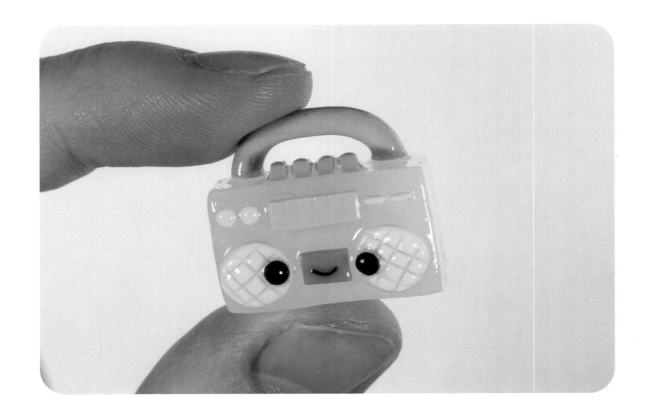

Boombox

The second installment in the electronics and objects category is a colorful little retro bombox. Stereos and boomboxes aren't things you see nowadays, but I wanted to include something from my childhood in this book.

Supplies

- Scrap polymer clay
- Polymer clay blade
- Supplies needed to make a silicone mold (see page 14)
- Polymer clay in light blue, black, and pink
- UV or two-part resin
- Light pink pigment
- UV lamp (for UV resin or glaze, if used)
- Paintbrush or plastic stick

Make the Boombox Template

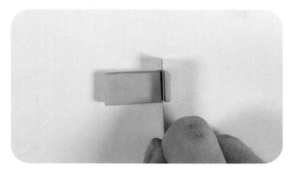

1. Pinch some clay into a rectangular cube shape. Using a polymer clay blade, cut the ends to make the corners sharper and less rounded.

2. Bake the template according to the manufacturer's instructions, let it cool, and make a silicone mold.

Make the Boombox Details

1. To make each speaker, flatten a ball of light blue clay into a pancake shape. Use your clay blade to make indents in a crisscross pattern.

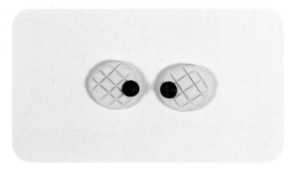

2. The speakers also serve as the eyes, so place a black dot on each speaker.

3. For the mouth, cut a small rectangle out of pink clay and place a little black smile on it. This is the little compartment where a cassette tape is inserted.

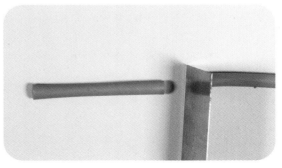

4. Roll some blue clay into a thick cylinder for the handle. Cut off the excess.

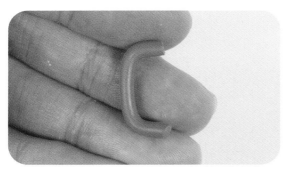

5. Bend the ends of the handle at 90-degree angles.

6. Use a blade to cut the ends of the handles to make sure they are equal lengths. Bake all the clay pieces according to the manufacturer's instructions. Allow them to cool.

Make the Resin Base

1. Pour a mixture of light pink pigment and resin into the silicone mold.

2. Let the resin cure, then carefully remove it from the mold so that you have a little pink rectangle to serve as the base.

Finish the Boombox

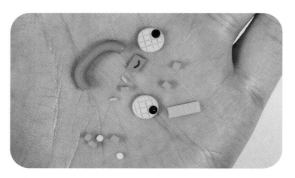

1. If you'd like, you can make little ovals, circles, squares, and rectangles out of clay for various buttons on the boombox.

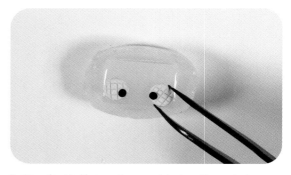

2. Now for the fun part: assembly. Lay the resin base flat and paint on a layer of resin all over the surface. Place the two speakers/eyes on the boombox.

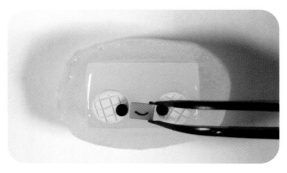

3. Attach the cassette compartment mouth.

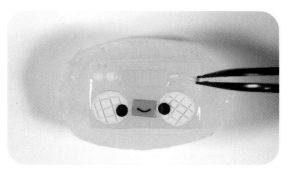

4. Add the optional buttons to fill up the space. Once all the buttons except for the orange squares are placed, allow the resin to cure.

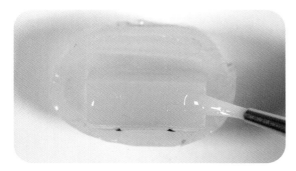

5. Rotate the cured boombox 90 degrees and apply resin to the top of the boombox.

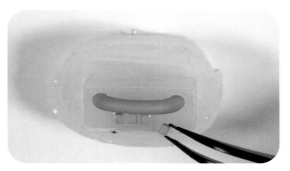

6. Attach the handle to the top of the boombox. Place the optional orange square buttons in front of the handle. After everything is set, cure completely. To finish, give the entire piece a resin glaze. Cure completely.

Television

Here's a staple electronic that I don't think I can live without: a television. Instead of a LED flat-screen smart TV, I decided to make a retro-style television. Similar to the alarm clock, this project doesn't need a silicone mold, but it does incorporate both resin and polymer clay.

Supplies

- Polymer clay in granite, red, silver, and black
- Clay roller
- Polymer clay blade
- UV or two-part resin
- UV lamp (for UV resin or glaze, if using)
- Paintbrush or plastic stick

Make the TV Screen & Frame

1. For a static TV screen, roll granite clay flat with a clay roller. (If you don't have any granite clay, you can add fine black glitter to gray clay.)

2. Use a polymer clay blade to cut out a rectangle.

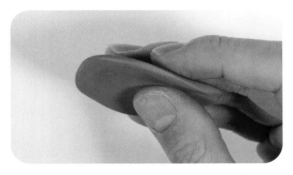

3. For the TV frame base, roll out a sheet of red clay, making sure it's somewhat thick.

4. Place the TV screen on the red clay, then set this aside until step 7.

5. Roll out another piece of red clay using the clay roller. Using a polymer clay blade, cut out a rectangle larger than the gray TV screen, which will be a tentative TV frame size. Make sure it's slightly larger than what you want it to be (in the next steps, you'll see why).

6. With a blade, cut out a rectangle that's smaller than the gray screen.

7. Place this rectangular TV frame on top of the screen and the larger sheet of red clay.

8. Trim the red layers to the desired size. This is why you made the initial frame a bit larger than desired, for the second cut: Cutting with the blade blends the edges together so you don't have to smooth them together.

Make and Add the TV Details

1. Old TVs usually have some sort of speaker or maybe a vent in the front. To represent that, cut a gray rectangle and make parallel indents with your blade. Place it on the bottom right side of the TV.

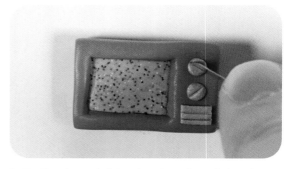

2. For the channel dials, place two silver circles above the speaker. Make indents across the center of each dial with a clay blade.

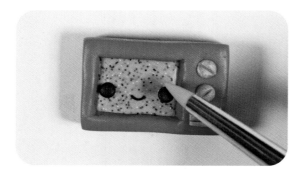

3. Add a face (see page 23) for extra cuteness.

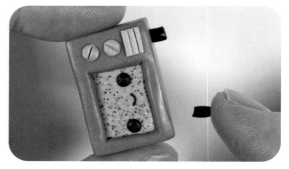

4. For the TV's legs, roll a thick snake of black clay and cut it into two equal cylinders. Place the legs on the bottom of the TV frame.

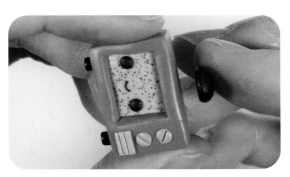

5. For the antenna base, make a little black dome by squishing a ball of black clay on a flat surface. Center it on top of the TV.

6. Make two little teardrop shapes from black clay for the antennae. Place them on the black dome, making them look almost like bunny ears.

7. Bake the TV according to the manufacturer's instructions. Once it has cooled, pour resin onto the TV screen, giving it a domed look. Cure completely. Finish the rest of the TV with a layer of resin glaze. Cure completely.

Rocket Ship

This next tutorial takes the electronic category into outer space. You'll make a little rocket ship using a silicone mold for the resin base and polymer clay details.

Supplies

- Scrap polymer clay
- Polymer clay blade
- Supplies needed to make a silicone mold (see page 14)
- Polymer clay in silver, red, orange, light blue, and black
- UV or two-part resin
- UV lamp (for UV resin or glaze, if using)
- Pearlescent pigment
- Super glue

Make the Rocket Body

1. Roll a ball of scrap clay into a cylinder.

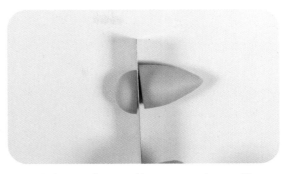

2. Pinch the tip of one end into a cone shape with your fingers. Using a polymer clay blade, cut off the excess.

3. Bake the template according to the manufacturer's instructions, let it cool, and then use it to make a silicone mold.

4. Make a mixture of pearlescent pigment and resin. Pour the pearly resin into the mold and cure completely before removing the rocket body from the mold.

Make the Rocket Details

1. For the bottom of the rocket, roll silver clay into a thick cylinder and cut a single slice out of it.

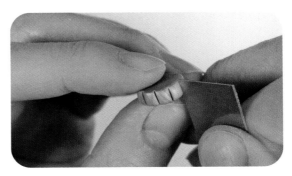

2. Using a clay blade, make parallel indents all around the sides of the silver disk.

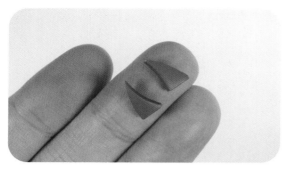

3. For the wings on the sides of the rocket, cut out two skinny isosceles triangles from red clay. Press the wings along the sides of the rocket body template to give them its natural curve, which will make it easier to fit them to the resin base later.

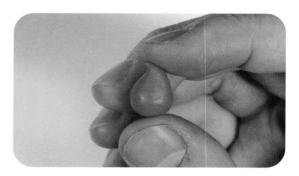

4. Next, make the flame that sticks out of the rocket. Pinch some red clay into a three-dimensional teardrop shape. Bend the tip of the teardrop shape to the side.

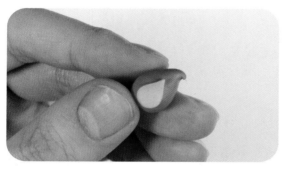

5. Make another teardrop shape in orange clay, but make it smaller and flat. Place it on top of the red flame.

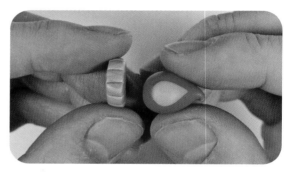

6. Attach the flame to the silver rocket bottom.

7. Make a small window to look out into space. Flatten a little light blue ball of clay into a pancake with a finger.

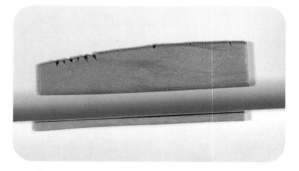

8. Roll out a sheet of silver clay and cut a thin strip.

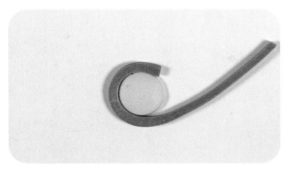

9. Wrap the thin strip around the outer edge of the light blue window. Cut off the excess clay and smooth the ends together. If you wish, make a separate little face out of black clay (see page 23).

10. Once all the clay details are finished, bake them according to the manufacturer's instructions. Allow them to cool.

Finish the Rocket

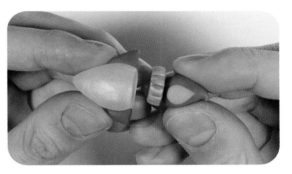

1. Apply super glue to the wings of the rocket and fit them to the sides of the resin body.

2. Glue on the rocket bottom with the flame.

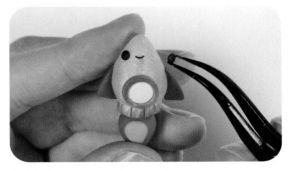

3. Attach the window between the two rocket wings.

4. Add the little face, if you made one, on the pointy part of the rocket, above the window. With a layer of completely cured resin glaze, the rocket ship is shiny and glimmering, just in time for its space expedition.

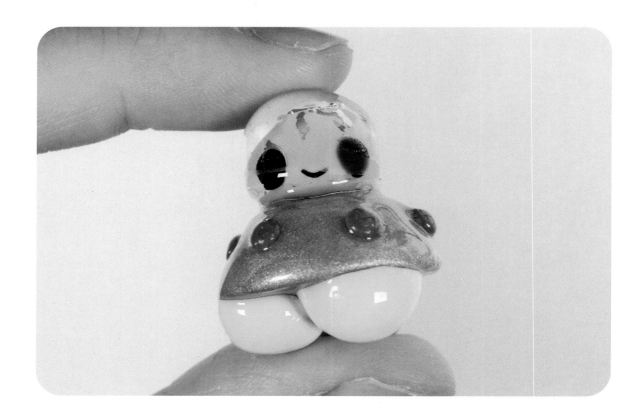

UFO

As we take our little rocket ship into space, we see an unidentified life force zipping by: a little alien in its tiny spaceship. This UFO includes a polymer clay base with a resin dome for the alien ship's window.

Supplies

- Scrap polymer clay
- Polymer clay blade
- Supplies needed to make a silicone mold (see page 14)
- Polymer clay in light green, silver, light yellow, blue, and black
- UV or two-part resin
- UV lamp (for UV resin or glaze, if used)
- Paintbrush or plastic stick

Make the Dome Template

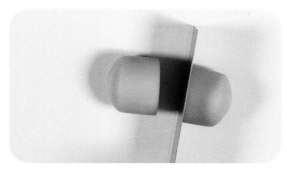

1. Roll a ball of clay into a large oval. Using a polymer clay blade, cut off one end of the oval. It should look like a little dome.

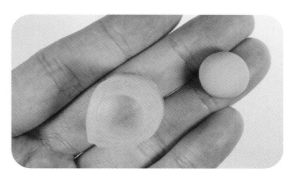

2. Bake the dome template according to the manufacturer's instructions. Once the template has cooled, use it to make a silicone mold.

Make the UFO Details

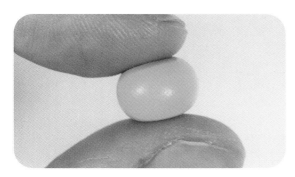

1. To make the little alien head, slightly squish a ball of light green clay.

2. Then give it two really large eyes and a smile from black clay.

3. To make the UFO ship, flatten a ball of silver clay with your finger.

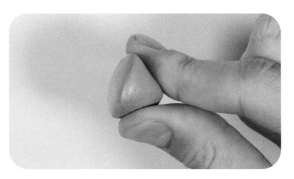

4. Pinch the top into a cone shape.

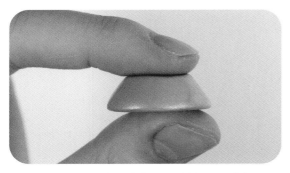

5. With a polymer clay blade, cut off the tip of the cone. You're only going to need the base part of the cone.

6. Cartoon UFO saucers always have little domes beneath that shine down beams of light. To make those little domes, cut a ball of light yellow clay in half.

7. Repeat with an identical ball of yellow clay. Add three of the domes to the bottom (larger) side of the silver saucer.

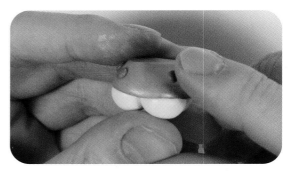

8. For a bit more decoration, add little blue dots of clay all around the saucer.

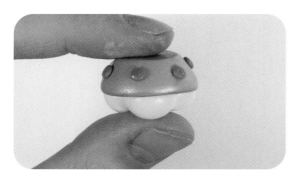

This is what the saucer should look like at this point.

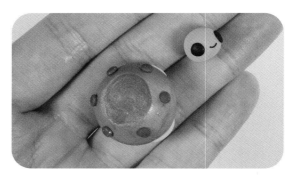

9. Bake the clay alien head and saucer according to the manufacturer's instructions. Allow them to cool.

Make the Resin Dome & Finish the UFO

1. Add only a little bit of resin into the dome mold so it's only about one-fourth to one-third full. Cure completely.

2. After the small layer of resin is cured, place the alien head upside down into the mold and fill the rest of the mold with resin. Then let the resin cure.

3. After the alien dome is cured, apply super glue to the bottom.

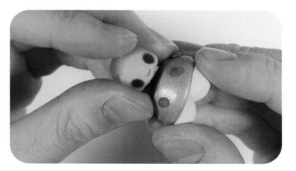

4. Place the dome on top of the clay saucer. Brush on a layer of resin glaze and cure completely. Note that air bubbles may get trapped in the resin when the alien head is placed, which happened with this alien UFO.

6

Kawaii

Food

Tutorials

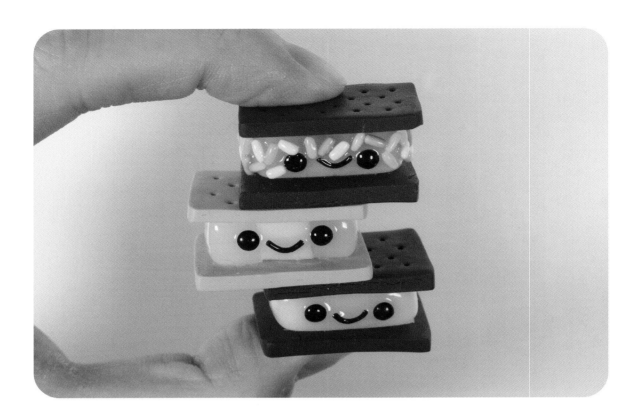

Ice Cream Sandwiches

The tutorials have moved from nature to marine life to animals to electronics, all the way to my favorite subject: food. The first project in this category is one I love—ice cream sandwiches. These cute treats have resin centers surrounded by polymer clay.

Supplies

- Scrap polymer clay
- Polymer clay blade
- Supplies needed to make a silicone mold (see page 14)
- Polymer clay in brown, tan, black, and pastel colors
- Clay roller
- Dotting tool
- UV or two-part resin
- Opaque white, opaque pink, and opaque green pigments
- UV lamp (for UV resin or glaze, if used)
- Super glue
- Paintbrush or plastic stick

Make the Ice Cream Templates

1. For the first ice cream template, pinch scrap clay into a rounded rectangular shape.

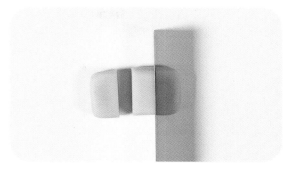

2. For the second ice cream template, make a rectangle similar to the first and cut it into three equal pieces.

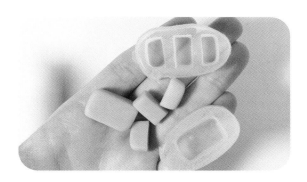

3. Bake the templates according to the manufacturer's instructions. Let them cool, and then use them to make silicone molds.

Make the Ice Cream Details

1. For the cookie part of the ice cream sandwich, roll out a sheet of brown clay.

2. Place the first ice cream template on the brown clay. Cut out a rectangle that's slightly larger than the template.

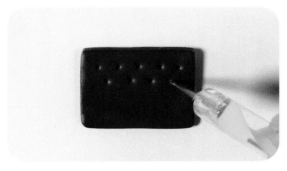

3. Use a dotting tool to make tiny little dots in offset rows in the brown rectangle.

4. Repeat steps 1-3 to make a total of six dotted rectangles in your choice of brown or tan clay. Bake them according to the manufacturer's instructions. Let them cool.

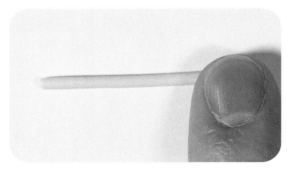

5. As an optional step, make some sprinkles by rolling out a thin snake of pastel-colored clay.

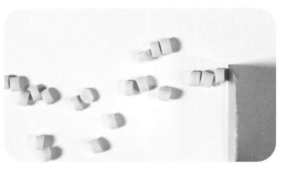

6. Cut the snake into small pieces, all the same size.

7. Use your fingers to roll the cut pieces into tiny ovals.

8. After making a bunch of sprinkles in other pastel colors, and optional faces for your sandwiches (see page 23), bake them according to the manufacturer's instructions. Let them cool.

Make the Resin Ice Creams & Finish the Sandwiches

1. Make three different mixtures of resin and pigment: one with opaque white, one with opaque pink, and one with opaque green.

2. For the first ice cream sandwich, pour just the opaque white resin into the full rectangle mold; cure completely.

3. Once it's cured, carefully remove it from the mold. Repeat to make another white resin ice cream.

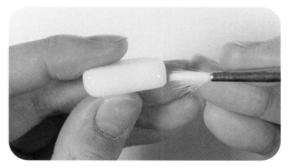

4. Apply a layer of resin on the sides of one of the ice cream centers.

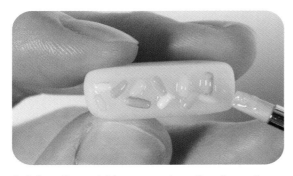

5. Adhere the sprinkles you made earlier all over the sides.

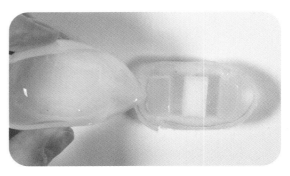

6. For the final ice cream center, pour each color of resin into the second mold, with the green and pink on the sides and the white in the center. Cure completely.

7. Carefully remove these pieces from the mold. I originally intended for this to be a Neapolitan ice cream sandwich, but I didn't have any brown pigment for the chocolate layer. So I settled for spumoni with a pistachio layer instead.

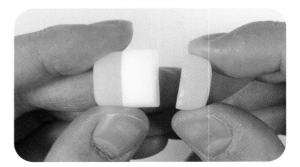

8. Apply super glue to the ice cream components and glue them together.

9. If you like, give faces to all of your ice cream sandwiches: the regular, the sprinkled, and the spumoni.

10. After applying super glue to the cookies (making sure it's not on the sides with the dots), attach them to the ice cream centers. To finish, apply resin glaze only to the ice cream centers, leaving the cookie parts matte. Cure completely.

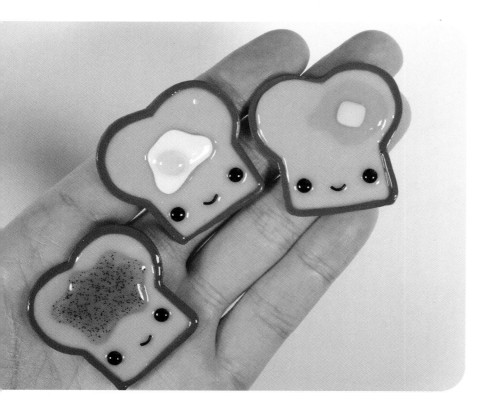

Supplies

- Polymer clay in tan, brown, white, yellow, and black
- Clay roller
- Paper for a template
- Polymer clay blade
- UV or two-part resin
- Yellow and red pigments
- UV lamp (for UV resin or glaze, if used)
- Black glitter
- Paintbrush or plastic stick

Breakfast Toast

Toast is a staple for a well-balanced breakfast. Here you'll make three varieties. This project doesn't use a silicone mold, but it still incorporates both polymer clay and resin.

Make the Toast Slices

1. Roll out a thin sheet of tan clay with a clay roller.

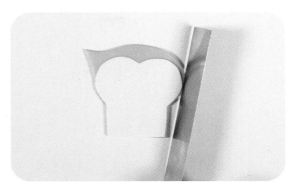

2. Cut out the toast shape. You can cut it out free-hand or use a paper template (basically a square with two circles on top), as shown.

3. Use your fingers to smooth any sharp corners on the rounded areas.

4. To make the crust, roll a long snake of brown clay, flatten it with a clay roller, then use a blade to cut a thin strip.

5. Wrap the strip of brown clay around the edge of the toast. Cut off the excess, and blend together the two ends of the strip.

6. Use black clay to add two eyes and a mouth near the bottom of the toast. Repeat steps 1-6 to make two more toasts.

Make Toast with a Fried Egg

1. To make the egg white, pinch a small white sheet of clay into a rounded organic shape.

2. Plop the egg white in the center of the toast.

3. For the yolk, place a small, flat, yellow circle of clay on the egg white. Bake according to the manufacturer's instructions. Let it cool, and then finish with a layer of resin glaze. Cure completely.

Make Buttered Toast

1. To make a pat of butter, pinch a small amount of yellow clay into a flat square shape. Plop the butter onto the toast, slightly off-center.

2. Bake according to the manufacturer's instructions. Let cool completely. Spread a mixture of resin and yellow pigment on top of the butter to make it look as if the butter is melting. Once the resin has cured, apply a layer of resin glaze. Cure completely.

Make Toast with Strawberry Jam

1. Cure a plain piece of toast; let cool. Starting in the center of the toast, spread on a mixture of red resin and fine black glitter to mimic the look of strawberry jam with seeds.

2. Spread the resin and glitter mixture toward the edges of the toast. Once the resin has cured, apply a layer of resin glaze. Cure completely.

Burger

Another of my favorite foods is a delicious hamburger. The buns here are made of resin using two clay templates and silicone molds, and the filling is made from polymer clay.

Supplies

- Scrap polymer clay
- Supplies needed to make a silicone mold (see page 14)
- UV or two-part resin
- Yellow pigment
- UV lamp (for UV resin or glaze, if used)
- Polymer clay in brown, yellow, green, red, and black
- Dotting tool
- Super glue
- Paintbrush or plastic stick

Make the Bun

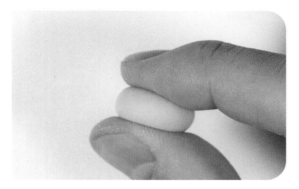

1. This project uses two different templates for the top and bottom buns of the hamburger. For the top bun, squish a ball of clay slightly between your fingers.

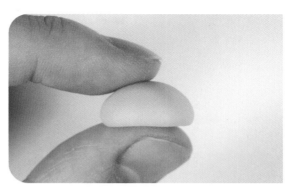

2. Place the bun on a flat surface. Press down on the perimeter to make a dome shape.

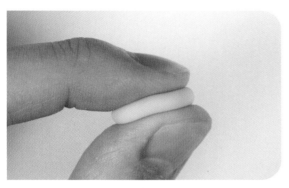

3. For the bottom bun, squish a ball of clay into a flat pancake.

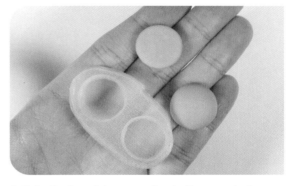

4. Bake the templates according to the manufacturer's instructions, let them cool, and then use them to make silicone molds.

5. Pour a mixture of yellow pigment and resin into both molds. Cure completely.

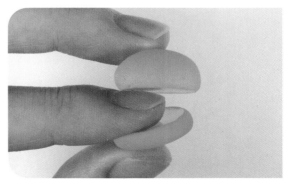

6. Remove the two resin bun halves from the mold.

Make the Clay Burger & Toppings

1. For the burger, squish brown clay into a rounded pancake shape.

2. Use a dotting tool to make multiple texture indents all over the burger.

3. Every burger needs its cheese. Flatten some yellow clay with a clay roller.

4. Cut it into a square shape.

5. Place the cheese on the burger and bend the corners downward to give it that melted cheese look.

6. To give your burger lettuce, flatten an oval piece of green clay.

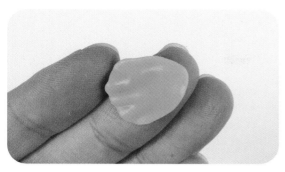

7. Bend one side of the lettuce into a ribbon pattern to resemble a lettuce leaf.

8. Plop the lettuce on top of the cheese.

9. Make two flat, red circles for tomatoes. Place them on top of the lettuce. Gently press all the clay pieces together.

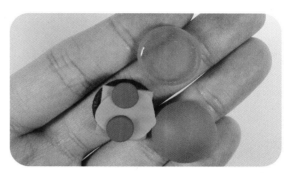

10. Bake the burger ingredients, along with the face pieces (see page 23), according to the manufacturer's instructions. Allow to cool.

Finish the Burger

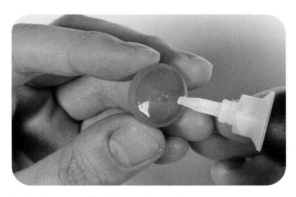

1. Apply super glue to one burger bun.

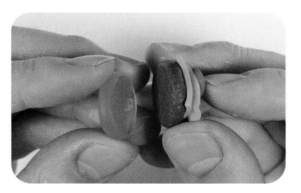

2. Press the clay burger content to the bun until the glue dries.

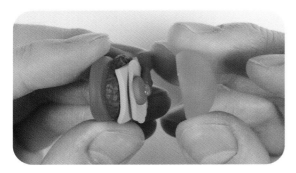

3. Repeat for the other bun.

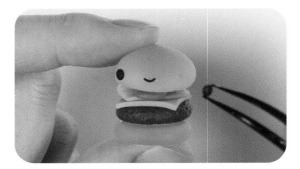

4. Give the burger a face. Apply a final layer of glaze and let it cure to complete this little burger. I don't know if I can eat a burger this cute.

Sushi Rolls

In this food tutorial, you will make two sushi rolls, or maki: a tuna roll and a cucumber roll. This project uses silicone molds, resin, and polymer clay.

Supplies

- Scrap polymer clay
- Polymer clay blade
- Supplies needed to make a silicone mold (see page 14)
- UV or two-part resin
- Red and green pigment
- UV lamp (for UV resin or glaze, if used)
- Polymer clay in translucent white, black, and white
- Clay roller
- Clear packing tape
- Paintbrush or plastic stick

Make the Tuna & Cucumber Templates & Resin Pieces

1. For the tuna template, roll scrap clay into a thick cylinder shape.

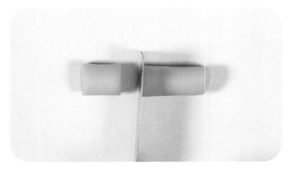

2. Using a polymer clay blade, cut off the ends of the cylinder.

3. For the cucumber template, roll a thick cylinder and cut two slices at an angle, to achieve a "pizza slice" look.

4. Make sure the tuna and cucumber templates are similar sizes and lengths. Bake the templates according to the manufacturer's instructions, let them cool, and then use them to make silicone molds.

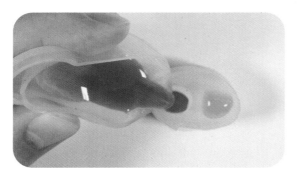

5. Pour a mixture of red pigment and resin into the circular mold for the tuna. Pour a green resin mixture into the triangular mold for the cucumber.

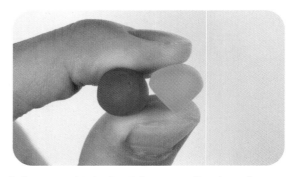

6. Cure completely. Carefully remove the pieces from the molds.

Make the Sushi Details

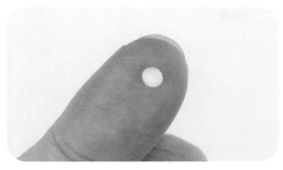

1. To make the little rice grains, start with a small ball of white translucent clay.

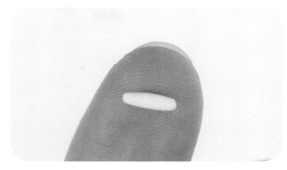

2. Roll the ball into an oval shape.

3. Repeat this step until you have a bunch of rice. Bake them according to the manufacturer's instructions. Let them cool.

4. To make the seaweed, roll black clay into a thick snake, then flatten it out with a roller, making sure it has a bit of thickness to it. If it's too thin, the seaweed won't retain its shape and may collapse on itself when we make the roll.

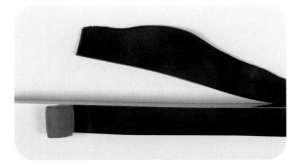

5. With your blade, cut out a rectangular strip from the black clay, measuring against the resin pieces to keep the heights the same.

6. Bend the seaweed strip into a circle.

7. Smooth the ends together with your fingers. Repeat for the second roll. Bake the seaweed rings according to the manufacturer's instructions, then allow them to cool.

8. Place a piece of packing tape sticky side up on a flat surface. Put both seaweed rings on the tape and gently press down to seal the bottoms.

Finish the Sushi Rolls

1. Fill each seaweed roll one-fourth of the way with resin.

2. Place the resin cucumber in the middle of one seaweed roll and the resin tuna in the middle of the other.

3. Fill the remaining space with the clay rice. Cure completely.

4. After the resin is cured, remove the tape. I also gave the sushi rolls faces using white clay. Brush on a layer of glaze and cure completely.

Gingerbread Man

And here we have our final project, ending on a festive note. A cute little gingerbread man, this project uses a resin base with polymer clay details. You can customize this project, using whatever type of decorations you choose.

Supplies

- Scrap polymer clay
- Clay roller
- Paper for a template
- Scissors
- Polymer clay blade
- Blending tool
- Supplies needed to make a silicone mold (see page 14)
- UV or two-part resin
- UV lamp (for UV resin or glaze, if used)
- Opaque orange pigment
- Polymer clay in white, red, green, and black
- Paintbrush or plastic stick

Make the Resin Gingerbread Man

1. First, roll out some scrap clay with clay roller. Make sure you leave a bit of thickness to it.

2. Cut out a chubby little human paper pattern as a guide to cutting out the gingerbread man. Place the pattern on the clay and use a polymer clay blade to cut around it.

3. If the edges of the clay shape are sharp, use a blending tool and your fingers to smooth them out.

4. Bake the template according to the manufacturer's instructions. Let it cool, and then use it to make a silicone mold.

5. Mix a very small amount of opaque orange pigment with resin to create a light tan gingerbread color. Pour this mixture into the mold and cure completely.

6. Once the resin is cured, take it out of the mold.

Make the Gingerbread Details

1. For the icing, roll out white clay into a thin snake. Cut the snake into four strips.

2. If you'd like to give your gingerbread man a bow-tie, pinch some red clay into a flat teardrop shape. Repeat so that you have two. Place the two teardrops next to each other, pointed ends in.

3. In the middle where the two teardrops meet, place a small red dot of clay. Make face pieces from black clay (see page 23) and green clay dots for buttons.

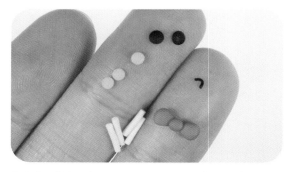

4. Bake all the clay components according to the manufacturer's instructions. Allow to cool.

Finish the Gingerbread Man

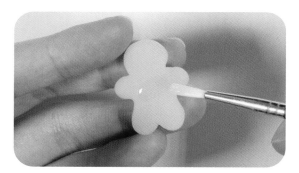

1. Apply a thin layer of resin to the resin gingerbread man.

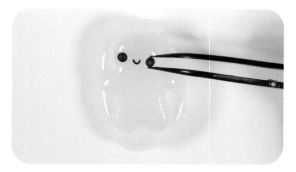

2. Add the face.

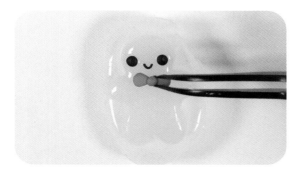

3. Place the bow next.

4. Attach the icing to the limbs.

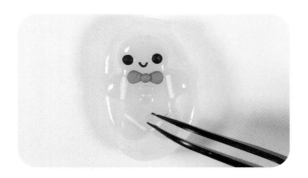

5. Finally, add the green buttons. Cure completely. Brush on a final layer of resin for a glazed finish. Cure completely.

Final Words

I hope you enjoyed all twenty-five tutorials in this book. It was definitely very rewarding for me to see all the different projects come to life. My goal was to include a mixture of different categories and different types of multimedia projects. Most importantly, I wanted to offer projects that serve as a basic foundation that you can build on and customize to reflect your own creativity.

I hope working on these projects inspires you to start your own crafting journey. Although there is a bit of an upfront investment in getting all the materials, the projects you'll create in the future make it all worth it. To me, crafting is a hobby and a method of relaxing, as well as a form of artmaking. I personally love imagining a sculpture and then creating it. There is something beautiful about making something with your own hands that began in your imagination.

Thank you for taking the time to read this book. If you make any of the projects, be sure to tag me on social media at #polymomotea so I can take a look.

Enjoy your crafting journey!

Resources

Tools & Supplies

Here's a list of some of the products I use to create the projects in this book. You can find many of them at your favorite retailers, both local brick-and-mortar craft and art supply stores as well as online. For a more complete list of tools and materials, see pages 11–12.

MOLDMAKING PRODUCTS
Sorta-Clear 12 Mold Maker:
www.smooth-on.com/products/sorta-clear-12

POLYMER CLAY
Fimo: www.staedtler.com/intl/en/products/fimo-modelling-clay-accessories

Sculpey: www.sculpey.com

TWO-PART RESIN
Alumite: www.alumilite.com/products/clear-resins

ArtResin: www.artresin.com

ETI EasyCast: www.eti-usa.com/easy-cast

Smooth-On Oomoo: www.smooth-on.com/product-line/oomoo

Unicone Art: www.unicone-art.com

UV RESIN
Signature Crafts: www.signaturecrafts.com/collections/resin-products

Solarez: www.solarez.com/product/solarez-clear-casting-uv-resin

FOR MORE RESIN INFORMATION & INSPIRATION
www.letsresin.com
www.resincraftsblog.com
www.resinobsession.com
www.sophieandtoffee.com

Where to Find PolymomoTea

FACEBOOK: www.facebook.com/polymomotea

INSTAGRAM: www.instagram.com/polymomotea

YOUTUBE: www.youtube.com/polymomotea

Acknowledgments

I would first like to thank my family, who always supported me in this hobby. They saw potential in my little creations even when I didn't think anything of it.

I would also like to give a shout-out to my close friends who basically idea-vomit different projects I should make when I say, "I need to think of something to make." So many great ideas came from them; without my good friends, there's no way this book could have been finished.

I would like to thank Joy for her guidance and the team at Quarry Books who helped make this book happen.

And finally, I would like to acknowledge all the creative souls out there who continuously create and support art. It is so inspiring to see the support and love from all the different artists, which makes it that much better to be a crafter.

About the Author

ALEX LEE was born in Chicago, Illinois, but moved to the Chicagoland suburbs at a young age. From there he went to university in Michigan and graduate school in Minnesota. Basically, he hopped from one cold state to the next, always regretting not going to school in Florida or Hawaii. Currently he is pursuing a career in dentistry and hopes to incorporate his love for craft into his work.

Alex, also known as PolymomoTea, started his crafting journey in 2014 by uploading a series of tutorials onto YouTube. He then spread his art to Instagram and the momentum grew from there. He started with just polymer clay, but then discovered UV resin a few years later and began to incorporate both materials into his projects.

Index